I0150879

THE FIRE OF LOVE

REFLECTIONS ON THE SPIRITUALITY OF JOHN OF THE CROSS

LEONARD DOOHAN

Copyright © 2019 by Leonard Doohan

All rights reserved.

All quotations of St. John of the Cross are taken from *The Collected Works of St. John of the Cross*, translated by Kieran Kavanaugh and Otilio Rodriguez Copyright © 1964, 1979, 1991 by Washington Province of Discalced Carmelites ICS Publications 2131 Lincoln Road, N.E. Washington, DC 20002-1199 U.S.A. www.icspublications.org Used with permission.

ISBN 13 978-1-7324777-1-1

ABBREVIATIONS OF THE WORKS OF JOHN OF THE CROSS

A = Ascent of Mount Carmel
N = Dark Night
C= Spiritual Canticle
F = Living Flame
P = Poetry
S = Sayings of Light and Love
Pr = Precautions
L = Letters

The Author

Dr. Leonard Doohan is Professor Emeritus at Gonzaga University, Spokane. He has written 27 books and many articles and has given hundreds of workshops and conferences throughout the USA, Canada, Europe, Australia, New Zealand, and Asia. Doohan's recent books include *Spiritual Leadership: the Quest for Integrity* (2007), *Enjoying Retirement: Living Life to the Fullest* (2010), *Courageous Hope: The Call of Leadership* (2011), *The One Thing Necessary: The Transforming Power of Christian Love* (2012), *Spiritual Leadership: How to Become a Great Spiritual Leader—Ten Steps and a Hundred Suggestions* (2014), *Ten Strategies to Nurture Our Spiritual Lives* (2014), *Rediscovering Jesus' Priorities* (2014), *and Growth in Christian Faith: Struggles, Glimpses of Grace, Life and Fulfillment (2018).* Doohan has given courses and workshops on John of the Cross all over the world.

Ten of Leonard Doohan's previous books on biblical spirituality and the spirituality of the laity have been republished by Wipf and Stock and are available at *wipfandstock.com*

Visit leonarddoohan.com

Books on the writings and spirituality of St. John of the Cross by Leonard Doohan:

The Contemporary Challenge of John of the Cross, 1995.

John of the Cross: Your Spiritual Guide, 2013.

The Dark Night is Our Only Light: A Study of the Book of the *Dark Night* by John of the Cross, 2013.

John of the Cross—The Spiritual Canticle: The Encounter of Two Lovers. An Introduction to the Book of the *Spiritual Canticle* by John of the Cross, 2013.

John of the Cross: *The Living Flame of Love*, 2014.

A Year with St. John of the Cross: 365 Daily Readings and Reflections, 2015.

See also The Contemporary Challenge of St. Teresa of Avila, 2016.

These books are available from amazon.com

Table of Contents

PREFACE

I first came in contact with the writings of John of the Cross in the 1970's when I had the opportunity to attend classes from several of the greatest scholars of John at the time, especially the Carmelite friar Federico Ruiz Salvador. His writings were considered to be among the greatest contributions to our understanding of John of the Cross and still are. Since most of his works were not translated, he is known in the USA as the editor and principal contributor of the beautiful tabletop book, *God Speaks in the Night*. Although at the time, my prime interest was the spirituality of laity in the Church, especially after the Second Vatican Council, I was so impressed with the breadth and rigor of Fr. Ruiz' approach to theology that I asked him to direct my doctoral dissertation. This gave me opportunity to spend time with him, to take his courses on John's theology and spirituality, and to learn as much as I could about John of the Cross. I also developed an enthusiasm for John of the Cross as one of the greatest exponents of Christian spirituality. I have given much of my time since to studying John, have given courses and conferences on his works all over the world, and have written six books on John of the Cross' principal works, his theology, and spirituality. Along with Francis of Assisi and Francis of Sales, I consider John of the Cross as one of the greatest exponents of Christian Spirituality and as one of the most relevant spiritual guides for today. These three, more than most, could transform our world.

In this current set of reflections I attempt to focus on the central aspect of all John's works. He is known for his teachings on the dark night, his insights into faith, his views of the stages of the spiritual life, his profound analysis of the place of the three theological virtues in human growth, his enthusiastic and positive understanding of creation as a reflection of God, and so on. John of the Cross is also known for his challenging approach to spiritual growth and some commentators even call him "doctor del las nadas" (the doctor of the nothings) because of his presumed rigorous rejection of all that is not God. But the Church has proclaimed him the "Mystical Doctor," and appreciates him as the great teacher of human and divine love and contemplation. When all is said and done, John is one of the greatest teachers the world has ever known on the importance of love as the central value and meaning of life, and this is the focus of my current reflections. I have chosen to leave aside the details, history, and analysis of his many works to center my thought on his teachings on love. He teaches us about "the great God of love," telling us "He whom my soul loves is within me," and "nothing is obtained from God except by love." He challenges us to make the journey to God, "along the spiritual road that leads to the perfect union with God through love." Wisely he tells us that we have to travel "with no other light or guide than the one that burns in our hearts," for it is "love alone that makes us soar to God," for this needs to be "a journey of strong love." There comes a point in this journey when we can say "nor have I any other work now that my every act is love," because we know that "when evening comes we will be examined on love." So, since "the ultimate reason for everything is love," let us be careful and "where there is no love put love, and we will draw out love." At the end of our journey, perhaps we can say with John "stricken by love, I lost myself and was found."

This present book depends a lot on material in my previous books. I have used ideas and material taken from those books but focused everything on the one great theme of John's teaching on love. John has made many significant contributions to spirituality that readers can be overwhelmed by the depth and extent of his works. Here I leave aside all other items to concentrate on the major topic that underlines all his teachings, namely the centrality of love. Readers interested in other aspects of his teaching can refer to my other books on the writings, theology, and spirituality of John of the Cross.

Chapter 1
John of the Cross—An example of love for us all

John—a prophet of God's love

John—teacher of divine and human love

John—guide on the journey to greater love

John—visionary of love for the world

John of the Cross lived from 1542 until 1591. He had very clear goals for what he wanted to achieve in life, namely the ultimate state of human, Christian maturity available to any man or woman—in other words the perfection of love towards God and all men and women. For John this is the purpose of life and the only commitment that gives meaning to our existence in this world. He pursued his goal no matter the situations he encountered, no matter the pain and sacrifice he needed to endure. He single-mindedly and single-heartedly sought to redirect the whole of his life to attain union with God in love, and his life evidenced a commitment to always choose what was the most loving thing to do. From early childhood through years of education and spiritual formation he prepared himself, and let God prepare him, to attain the quality of life he sought. He accepted hardship as he relentlessly pursued a life of love and union with God. He is an exceptional example for all of us in the quest for the meaning of life and finding it in love.

John's early life already showed traces of values that were to make up the general direction of his future. He saw, in the example of his parents, what it meant to sacrifice all for the sake of true love. The poverty of his family showed him that mere accumulation of things does not guarantee love and happiness. However, the pain and struggles that came with poverty made John sensitive to deprivation in others and always ready to alleviate it where he could. His family fostered piety, and John treasured such attitudes throughout his life. Compassionate charity, learned especially in his hospital service, became a permanent feature in his concern for others. At considerable personal sacrifice, John always integrated study into his life, from the early years in the Jesuit university of Medina del Campo right up to his last years in Andalusia. Deep love for God and for others was the special quality that permeated John's whole life, as it did his message. Poverty, charity, piety, study, authenticity, and deep love formed permanent parts of John's life.

John was a man of destiny. From his early life, when friends had all kinds of plans for him, he had a clear picture of what he wanted from life. He had a sense of vocation—he felt personally called by God to pursue love in every aspect of life. He worked in the hospital, was successful, enjoyed the work, but knew there is more to life than generous, successful ministry. He went to the Jesuit school in Medina, thoroughly enjoyed study and valued it all his life, but recognized that for him there had to be more to life than education. Entering the Order of Mount Carmel, attracted by its spirit of contemplation, he had a happy novitiate and learned to encounter God in new ways. But this experience too, great as it was, did not satisfy John's yearning for a life of love and union with God. He then went to Salamanca for theology, a chance to study about God, but no amount of study alone led him to union with God. He decided to join the Carthusians, but Teresa of Avila encouraged him to seek the deeper contemplative union he wanted in her renewed Carmel. By the age of 25, John had learned that ministry, education, religious life, and theology do not automatically insure knowledge of and union with God. Even reforming an institution to facilitate the life one seeks is no guarantee. John sensed an irresistible attraction to God and pursued this goal uncompromisingly and relentlessly. What he had experienced he valued but, without despising previous experiences, he left them aside to continue the search for total love in new ways.

Some people accumulate many small manifestations of love for God. Others make a single-minded, single-hearted choice for love of God, and see everything as secondary to the quest for God's love. So much love today is at best believed-in love and leads now and again to small gestures of love. This kind of accumulated love rarely implies renunciation; whereas love that flows from a fundamental and deliberate choice to direct one's entire life to God always does. In choice-oriented love the seeker renounces all that up to the present was viewed as the best means available, renounces without despising previous means, and moves forward to the goal of a life centered on love. Choice-love is creative of one's personality, as is evident in John, who sought God even through the nights, journeying to the union for which he yearned. Accumulated small expressions of love never substitute for choice-oriented love, even though they may help to manifest and maintain it. Choice-oriented love—love that is a manifestation of one's fundamental, unwavering option in life—is the clearest indicator of ongoing conversion, while accumulated love can still be shown by someone who refuses to face the need for a total conversion and transformation. When you read the life of John of the Cross you cannot help but be filled with sadness, joy, peace, and a sense of wonder and awe. Reading his life is exciting. John integrated all the best values from his experience in one great thrust of self-dedication to the love of God. His goal was always clear, never neglected or watered down, and he pursued it with the united effort of all his strength, talents, and unified affectivity. His was not a selfish goal of personal growth, for he took others along with him, sharing the vision and the love by which he felt drawn. John's message is exemplified in his life which is based on love, focused on love, and dedicated to the priority of love in every decision he made.

John—a prophet of God's love

We often mistakenly think a prophet speaks about the future, but this function is minor and accidental to the biblical prophet's main task. The word "prophet" comes from Greek and means to speak on behalf of God. A prophet challenges people to live in the present according to the values of God, and surely there are few people to whom this applies more than John of the Cross. The influences on his life were at times unusual, but he pursues his goal of union with God in love no matter the circumstances. At times his was a voice in the wilderness proclaiming the wonders of God and calling all to faithfully pursued transformative union even through the nights of life. Like any great prophet John was unrelenting in proclaiming God's message to the world—a message that gives priority to love over all else.

John lived with many people who had a wrong set of values, whether they were political leaders who saw greatness in expansionism, wars, power, and wealth, or religious leaders forcing conversions, controlling other people's belief, and imposing their own views on others. Likewise the social caste system of his day stressed wealth, status, and bloodlines as important aspects of life. John lived with people who were attached to the structures and pseudo values that gave them power and prestige. He understood how useless it was to force belief systems on people who did not want them. All around him he saw people creating God in their own image and likeness, unwilling to let go of their created god and let God be a transforming presence in their lives. A prophet condemns such warped views of humanity and religion and challenges us to follow God, for faith needs to be a loving self-gift. John does that! John is a prophet who denounces injustice, oppression, greed, and all forms of selfishness and lack of love.

John was poor in spirit, or even more, poor with spirit. He loved being poor and appreciated how this gave him a perspective on life that he otherwise would never have. He lived peacefully in spite of religious corruption all around him. In fact, he always lived with love for the Church with its awkwardness and with its graciousness. He knew that even bad situations have potentiality for good, and he sought such goodness amidst the horrors inflicted on him. It is amazing how John kept focused on his goals of union with God no matter the circumstances around him. His life was a prophetical statement of God's love. But, he was practical too, and knew when enough was enough; so he knew when it was time to escape from the prison that the religiously arrogant had created for him.

As a prophet of God, John above all told us how to see God's love everywhere, in nature, in people, and even in oppressors. John appreciated his own enduring purpose in life, his own destiny. He yearned for transformation in loving union with God. John pursued spiritual growth but never selfishly, rather always with a sensitivity and compassion towards everyone he met. He was not a lonely mystic in selfish pursuit of perfection. He was a man for others; enjoying others' company, facilitating their growth, and seeking whatever was best for them. More than anything, this prophet lived his life aware of a realm of life beyond this one that gave meaning to this one. No matter the situations of his day and the nights he had to live, John spoke of God's love and even reminds us the nights might be dark, but they can be guiding, transforming, and beautiful.

John—teacher of divine and human love

John of the Cross is unquestionably the mystical doctor of divine and human love, and we see this so well in his writings which treat of the entire spiritual life primarily from an affective perspective. They show us the growth of love from early anxieties and yearnings to God's illuminative guidance and teachings on love, and on to the in-breaking of God's love into the searching soul. They then proclaim the intensity of union between the lovers in mutual peace, surrender, and self-gift, and speak of the Lover's gift of equality in love. In the Toledo prison, John experienced mystical union in love and felt the urge to proclaim it in the verses of his poems and later to share them. Mystics long to share their experiences as a sign of their love for God whose love they experienced and in appreciation of the divine gifts they have received. They have a profound desire to express their experience and in doing so they enrich it and re-live it. John's teachings on love are not founded on what he has studied but on what he experienced of the love of God.

John's poems describe the trajectory of love from one who has experienced it, and John is not just a love-poet, but a lover. "[T]here is an abandonment to all the sensations of love, which seems to me to exceed, and on their own ground, in directness and intensity of spiritual and passionate longing, most of which has been written by love-poets of all ages. These lines, so full of rich and strange beauty, ache with desire and all the subtlety of love . . . this monk can give lessons to lovers."[1] At first, John was reluctant to write about this experience as he tells us in the *Living Flame*. "I have felt somewhat reluctant . . . to explain these four stanzas . . . . since they deal with matters so interior and spiritual, for which words are usually lacking . . . . I find it difficult to say something of their content" (F. Prologue.1; see also A. Prologue.1 and C. Prologue.2). Language is so important to us for communication, for development of relationships, and for our own growth as individual human beings. It is particularly important in matters of religion where we transmit vital experiences through the language of faith. Sometimes expressions of faith end up as just words, and we then lose the reality behind the words. John was concerned that the powerful experiences of love not be lost in mere words. Thus, John comments on the efforts of some who went before him. "The saintly doctors, no matter how much they have said or will say, can never furnish an exhaustive explanation of these figures and comparisons, since the abundant meanings of the Holy Spirit cannot be caught in words. Thus, the explanation of these expressions usually contains less than what they embody in themselves" (C. Prologue.1).

People who have had a profound spiritual experience generally find it difficult to explain it to others in precise language. Often this is because they do not fully understand it themselves, or their explanation always seems to fall far short of the experience. Sometimes they use symbolic or suggestive language to explain their experiences. John himself pointed this out; "everything I say is as far from reality as is a painting from the living object represented" (F. Prologue.1). Because of this difficulty, mystics often use figurative expressions rather than rational explanations. "These persons let something of their experience overflow in figures, comparisons, and similitudes, and from the abundance of their spirit pour out secrets and mysteries rather than rational explanations" (C. Prologue.1). John speaks about love with great enthusiasm and at times is overwhelmed by the exciting encounters of loving union.

Thus, John can also advise us: "As a result, though we give some explanation of these stanzas, there is no reason to be bound to this explanation. For mystical wisdom, which comes through love . . . need not be understood distinctly in order to cause love and affection in the soul, for it is given according to the mode of faith through which we love God without understanding him" (C. Prologue.2). He comments further: "It is better to explain the utterances of love in their broadest sense so that each one may derive profit from them according to the mode and capacity of one's own spirit, rather than narrow them down to a meaning unadaptable to every palate. As a result, though we give some explanation of these stanzas, there is no reason to be bound to their explanation" (C. Prologue.2). So, conceptual and speculative language may help to clarify and articulate our faith, but its vital core—our loving relationship with God—is more truly shared "in mystical theology which is known through love and by which these truths are not only known but at the same time enjoyed" (C.

Prologue.3). John's presentation of these matters is so profound he is recognized as the Mystical Doctor of divine and human love.

John—guide on the journey to greater love

The poem and commentary of the *Spiritual Canticle,* taken together, form one of the greatest treatises on love in all of spirituality. It presents the spiritual journey as a progressive penetration into the depths of divine love, as a transformation in love, and as a realization that life is more set on love than anything else. God is the Spirit of love who raises us up in love, awakens us to the life of love, and inspires us to love more. God steals our hearts for love, enkindles love within us, moves us to freely love God, and rejoices in the love we show. John speaks about love as the all-embracing aspect of our relationship to God: he speaks of the spirit of love, utterances of love, wisdom of love, detachment of love, darkness of love, friendship of love, and knowledge of love. Every aspect of life is touched and transformed by love. John describes the love with which God transforms the soul as rigorous, intense, impatient, tender, burning, and ardent. This love is vehement, sweet, delightful, intimate, and lofty. It is fortified, inebriating, supreme, generous, pure, solitary, and interior. It is also savory, strong, mighty, indescribable, glorious, and eventually painless. This love is a festivity, it is mutual, enflames the soul, fills her with fervor, refreshes and renews, and gradually produces likeness with the Lover. What extraordinary vocabulary John uses in dealing with love! We certainly have an exciting guide!

In the early stages of her pursuit of her Lover, the bride in the *Spiritual Canticle* says she is wounded with love, longs for love, and seeks her Bridegroom with intense impatient love. She claims to truly love God, to have a lover's heart, to love him above all things, and even to feel she is dying with love. As she pursues a life of love and acts always through love, she gives herself totally in love and longs for the wages of this love. She lives in the condition of love, cries out for more love, and longs for love's completion. She feels refreshed and renewed in love, evidences the excesses of love, and makes a true "yes" of her love for her Bridegroom. As she enters spiritual marriage she longs to become perfect in loving her Bridegroom, and feels moved by love to love more. She is now absorbed in love, transformed in love, employs her entire being in loving, and does everything with love. She wants nothing for herself but desires to become like her Lover, as gradually her love becomes God's love.

These are John's descriptions of how one should pursue love from the breathless rush to love in the early phases, to the enjoyment of love and desire for more love, to the peaceful completion of love in union. When we read John's descriptions, we know there cannot be any appropriate ending to the story except that the two be together in a communion of love in which they give themselves to each other, keeping nothing back. Now the soul's total self-gift reflects God's total self-gift which has always been there drawing the soul throughout the journey. When John writes, he has already completed this journey and can guide us from his experience.

John—visionary of love for the world

John presents us with a wonderful and exciting understanding of the spiritual journey that we are all called to undertake. However, he does more than that; he gives us a vision for life in community, whether ecclesial or civil. He gives us a vision of love for the world. In one of his most famous sayings he reminds us, "When evening comes, you will be examined in love" (S. 60). In his *Romances* he outlined God's strategy of love for the world, and in his poems and major works he places before us our vocation to love. This is a hard journey filled with sacrifice, but humanity is not destroyed in this journey but reaches its full potential. Experiencing God's love is a learning situation for us.

In this journey we learn the importance of love in our experience of God's love for us. We see the example of love in God's approach to this world and to ourselves, and know the gift includes a challenge to live the love of faith. In thinking about God, scrutinizing and seeking answers to questions of belief and religion are not enough; we must transform ourselves by love. John teaches us that God is not known by what we think or by our arguments, no matter how persuasive we may think they are. Rather, we experience God in love, and we know God through lives based on love.

John points out that our experience forces us to take a stand and to live differently because we know we are loved. Our own awareness enables us to glimpse transcendent reality—that it is love that is the basis for life in this world and for life beyond the normal realms of experience. We cannot merely believe in the power of love, we must act on that conviction and show our dedication in action. This means making decisions based on the most loving thing to do.

As we grow in the spiritual life we change our own attitudes to life. We reject selfishness, greed, and self-satisfaction, and thus we move away from self-centeredness to self-transcendence. When we live in this way, we ourselves are the first focus of transformation. This is a rigorous self-training and eventually leads to the integration of all aspects of life in loving self-gift to God. This single-hearted pursuit of the way of love transforms our decisions, actions, and purposes in life. John's spirituality and vision of humanity is always practical, he focuses on men and women in need of transformation and he offers us a vision for the world—a vision of love.

As we begin our reflections on the centrality of love in the teachings of John of the Cross there can be no better point of departure than to reflect on the life and example of John himself. He is singularly engaged on the pursuit of love, exceptional among many such focused spiritual giants. He is a model of love for us all. In presenting love he has taken on the role of a prophet, speaking on behalf of God and declaring God's challenging message of love for all who will listen. John confronts a world without love, he shows how God's message of love gives comfort and hope to those who yearn for the transformation of love. He calls us all to rebuild our personal lives, our Church, and our world on God's vision of love. He then invites each of us to journey with him to greater love and to immerse ourselves in God's vision of love. For John the meaning of life was to be found in the pursuit of love, and he teaches us that it still is today.

Chapter 2
God—our model of love

God's life of love

God's world of love

God's invitations of love

John's understanding of God is the point of departure for his life and his ministry of spiritual direction and writing. His understanding of God's inner life as centered on love and of God's strategy of love in salvation history are best expressed in John's nine *Romances*. These beautiful poems serve as the point of departure for John's vision of life and act as a prologue to all his major works. He goes on to describe a beautiful vision of a world of love and shows us how the whole world is full of invitations to love. Truly God is our model of love.

God's life of love

The extraordinary love-filled *Romances* are an important part of John's theological vision, synthesizing his understanding of God's strategy of love in salvation history; God's plan for the world. They complement the disciple's return journey to God which John describes in his major works. These *Romances* are the point of departure for John's vision of life with God and act as a prologue to all his other works. Everything John presents as our return journey to God is modeled on God's journey to us as described in these *Romances*. These nine ballads present poetical reflections on the Trinity, Incarnation, and humanity's redemption through love. One author appropriately describes them as "the Gospel of John of the Cross."[2] These beautiful poems portray the vision of the eternal life of God, the shared love in the intercommunication of the Trinity, their love-filled gift of creation, the incarnation, and Jesus' ministry of love. John presents the history of salvation as a project of love, overflowing from the Trinity's inner life of love. One commentator points out that these *Romances* "provide a wider narrative and doctrinal framework for San Juan's whole poetic enterprise, and link the passionate and sensuous encounter of the two lovers in the liras with the divine Trinity's embrace of all humanity through use of the same fundamental image, the marriage."[3]

The first *Romance* portrays the inner life of the Trinity in its eternal, atemporal, mutual loving. The three persons of the Trinity are bound together in eternal love, "an inexpressible knot." The eternal begetting of the Word is an act of love by the Father, and their sharing of love is the Holy Spirit, so that there is "one beloved among all three." This part of John's vision is foundational for the disciple's return journey to God.

> 1,v.6 As the lover in the beloved
> each lived in the other,
> and the Love that unites them
> is one with them,
>
> 1,v.7 Their equal, excellent as
> the One and the Other;
> three Persons, and one Beloved
> among all three.
>
> 1,v.8 One love in them all
> makes them one Lover,

and the Lover is the Beloved
in whom each one lives.

1,v.11 Thus it is a boundless
love that unites them,
for the Three have one love
which is their essence;
and the more love is one
the more it is love

The second *Romance* deals with the internal communication among the persons of the Trinity. It is a communication in love, already heralded as the basis for the Father's love of the Son's future disciples. The Father's love for the Son is so strong that He wishes to love all that the Son loves, and this sets up the basis for all future spirituality; "My Son, I will give myself to him who loves you, and I will love him with the same love I have for you, because he has loved you whom I love so." This is part of the dynamism of love that by its very nature always wants to extend itself.

2,v.1 In that immense love
proceeding from the two
the Father spoke words
of great affection to the Son,

2,v.3-4 " My Son, only your
company contents me,
and when something pleases me
I love that thing in you;
he who resembles you most
satisfies me most,

2,v.5 and whoever is like you in nothing
will find nothing in me.
I am pleased with you alone
O life of my life!"

2,v.7 My Son, I will give myself

> to him who loves you
> and I will love him
> with the same love I have for you,
> because he has loved
> you whom I love so."

The third *Romance* is a dialogue between Father and Son, the former wanting a bride for the Son, the latter wanting a bride who glorifies the Father.

> 3,v.1 "My Son, I wish to give you
> a bride who will love you.
> Because of you she will deserve
> to share our company,
>
> 3,v.5 I will hold her in my arms
> and she will burn with your love,
> and with eternal delight
> she will exalt your goodness."

This extension of love seems so right that in the fourth romance the Father proclaims, "Let it be done." This is the first reference to spiritual marriage as a reflection of the life of love in the Trinity—the bride is all creation. Thus, creation becomes a project of love between the Father and the Son, and the love we find in the world is the epiphany of God's love.

The promise of the fourth *Romance* continues the theme of creation. It portrays creation as a loving gift from Father to Son, a way in which the Father can love the Son even more. Creation is so overwhelmingly rich because of the Father's extraordinary love for the Son. The bride here refers to all creation, heavenly and earthly, that the Father intends as a gift of love to the Son, but whom the Son intends to return to the Father as a further sign of the Son's love. In this gamble of love by God, the Son is so desirous of showing the world how to love the Father that he decides to become part of the world himself.

4,v.1 "Let it be done, then," said the Father,
for your love has deserved it.
and by these words
the world was created,

4,v.10 for he would make himself
wholly like them,
and he would come to them
and dwell with them;

4,v.15 He would take her
tenderly in his arms
and there give her his love;
and when they were thus one,
he would lift her to the Father.

4.v.16 For as the Father and the Son
and he who proceeds from them
live in one another,
so it would be with the bride;
for, taken wholly into God,
she will live the life of God.

The promise of the fourth *Romance*, a promise of love, becomes the hope of the fifth and sixth, a hope portrayed in terms of the longings of humanity for God. John describes the world's yearnings and expectations for the transforming love of God. After all, God's dealings with the world are undertaken to awaken our love for God. This hope culminates in Simeon's recognition in the sixth romance of the light that descended from the heights.

The seventh and eighth *Romances* describe the Incarnation, in which the lover becomes like the one he loves. The Father urges the Son to become like his bride, and the Son responds in love to the Father by willing the Incarnation. The Father stresses the need for likeness to create perfect love between lovers, "that the lover becomes like the one he loves," a theme John will develop in the *Spiritual Canticle*. The eighth *Romance* concludes with the loving obedience of Mary.

7,v.5 that the lover become
like the one he loves;
for the greater their likeness
the greater their delight.

7,v.6 Surely your bride's delight
would greatly increase
were she to see you like her,
in her own flesh.

7,v.10 I will go seek my bride
and take her upon myself
her weariness and her labors
in which she suffers so;

7,v.11 And that she may have life,
I will die for her,
and, lifting her out of that deep,
I will restore her to you.

The ninth *Romance* brings the hope, the plan, and the promise into history through the revelation of the conception and birth through the mother, Mary. Thus, the Son comes to his bride and the world is turned upside down because of the love of the Father and the Son; "such an exchange; things usually so strange." This *Romance* concludes in the extraordinary betrothal of the baby by his mother to humanity; "Men sang songs and angels melodies celebrating the marriage of two such as these."

9,v.2 Embracing his bride,
holding her in his arms,
whom the gracious Mother
laid in a manger. . .

9,v.6 In God, man's weeping,,
and in man, gladness,
to the one and the other
things usually so strange.

There is a tenth *Romance*, a commentary on psalm 137, "By the waters of Babylon," which is not directly linked to the other nine, but it portrays the psalmist's pain, hope, and longing for God's deliverance and for salvation in Jesus. John writes this in the first person, and it becomes an appropriate expression of John's own love and longings for deliverance from his prison in Toledo. "I begged love to kill me. . . I died within myself for you."

> 10,v.14 And he will gather his little ones
> and me, who wept because of you,
> at the rock who is Christ
> for whom I abandoned you.

As the commentator says, these *Romances* form the gospel of John of the Cross, the good news that the world is redeemed and transformed by love.

God's world of love

In John's vision, the created world surrounds us with God's love. In the *Romances* the Father gives the world to the Son as a bride, and the Son transforms the world and re-gives it to the Father. Creation is a gesture of love between Father and Son that is then extended to men and women who have eyes to see the wonders of God. John loved the beauty of God's creation not just in general but with a particular appreciation for each one of God's creatures. There are four points to John's approach to creation. First, the temporal veil of all creatures must be renounced if one is to seek union with God. Creatures, in spite of their beauty, cannot become ends in themselves. "[I]n order to obtain union with God . . . all the things of the world are renounced, all natural appetites and affections mortified" (F. 1.29). John is not opposed to nature, but knows it can become a block to union with God when people are attached to and possessive of things. "If you purify your soul of attachments and desires, you will understand things spiritually. If you deny your appetite for them, you will enjoy their truth, understanding what is certain in them" (S. 49). At first, the person actively participates in this purification, but later it is achieved by the transforming love of the Trinity. "You detach and withdraw the soul from all the other touches of created things by the might of Your delicacy, and reserve it for and unite it to Yourself alone" (F. 2.18).

While John opposes attachment to anything other than God and any movement towards absolutizing one's desire for creatures instead of God, he loved the beauty of the world with a refinement never found in men and women who lack spiritual vision. In John's writings there is no sign of "flight from the world," as seen in so much piety. John views the world through a different lens than we often do, and so everything changes for him. Love made John see everything in a new way, in a real way. At the same time he realizes that everything around him is a gift of love, and all the world speaks of the presence of a loving God. John tells us that this revelation of God "produces a symphony of love in the world." It is like "a supper that refreshes and deepens love" (C. 14-15.27). So, we must look at the world with the eyes of faith, appreciating its beauty, but never letting any aspect of it to become an end in itself.

The second point in John's approach to creation is to appreciate that during the ascetical period of the spiritual journey creatures can lead us to God, for "the consideration of creatures is first in order after the exercise of self-knowledge" (C. 4.1). This is important for it helps us become aware of the greatness of God's love and generosity in creation and can thus awaken our love for God. "Only the hand of God, her Beloved, was able to create this diversity and grandeur" (C. 4.3). When John looks at the world in this way he concludes, "It seems [to the soul] that the entire universe is a sea of love in which it is engulfed, for, conscious of the living point or center of love within itself, it is unable to catch sight of the boundaries of this love" (F. 2.10). So, when we look at the world around us, we can see traces of God's presence in creatures, and we become "anxious to see the invisible beauty that caused this visible beauty" (C. 6.1). So, as we journey to God's love we learn to appreciate how God has lovingly transformed the whole world so that it now reveals the divine presence. Speaking of every aspect of the world, John says that God "having looked at them, with his image alone, clothed them in beauty" (C. 5). As one journeys onward, "the soul becomes aware of Wisdom's wonderful harmony and sequence in the variety of her creatures and works" (C. 14-15.25).

The third point in John's approach is when in contemplation all is transformed in God and we see God in every aspect of creation. "In that nocturnal tranquility and silence and in the knowledge of the divine light the soul becomes aware of Wisdom's wonderful harmony and sequence in the variety of her creatures and works" (C. 14-15.25). John helps us discover the inner world of God's love, and in the *Spiritual Canticle* he represents "a reordering of the cosmos, a world made new," and "we begin to see that world differently and sense something of its beauty and wonder."[4] Earlier in the spiritual journey creation was a reflection of God's beauty, later reflection moves to identification, "My Beloved, the mountains . . . . "

John's vision of love includes the conviction that we are surrounded by God's love. He abandons former spiritualities' negative approach to the world and focuses our attention on a renewed world. He challenges us to see the world differently than previously, to appreciate its beauty and wonder, and to realize all this is the result of God's love. At times this harmony of a world of love is shattered, and we see the destruction of the concept of love. There are so many people whose lives are filled with violence, untruthfulness, fear, hate, and oppression. They destroy creation with their wars, abuse, pollution and greed. Humanity has created its own hell on earth by driving love out of our lives. People around us, sometimes friends, and often ourselves, make unloving decisions that destroy us from within and ruin our world that was created by and for love. We evidence a lot of conscious and unconscious resistance to God's love and illumination. However, even when love is lacking, we always retain remembrance of the call to love that is integral to our personalities—creation pleads with us to remember. Sometimes we see love and it motivates us to appreciate our call; at other times our world cries out for love, and that, too, can motivate us to respond. God's love—our hope—overwhelms and overcomes the depressing misery of our world. While aware of life's problems, we must maintain a mature focus on love.

John steps from renunciation to seeing reflections of God's beauty in creation, to an appreciation of the sacramental quality of creation. He then moves on in the *Living Flame* to a wonderful conclusion, his fourth point, that a person knows creatures through God and not God through creatures. At this time we experience an awakening of the Word in the deepest part of our spirit, so that "all the virtues and substances and perfections and graces of every created thing glow and make the same movement all at once" (F. 4.4). Thus, "all things seem to move in unison," and "they all likewise disclose the beauties of their being, power, loveliness, and graces, and the root of their duration and life. For the soul is conscious of how all creatures, earthly and heavenly, have their life, duration, and strength in Him" (F 4.5).

John offers a wonderful conclusion, namely, that we now know all these created things better in God's being than in themselves. "And here lies the remarkable delight of this awakening: the soul knows creatures through God and not God through creatures" (F. 4.5). This is a reversal of our normal ways of thinking about these things: we know the effects through the cause and not the cause through the effects. This is a new supernatural vision of the relationship between God and creation. In this vision, a person "sees what God is in Himself and what He is in His creatures in only one view" (F. 4.7). This is a mystical vision of the cosmos, in which every creature has its place and meaning in the plan of God, for all creation is restored in God's transforming love. We live in a world of love.

God's invitations of love

The world is full of God's many invitations to appreciate divine love. The whole world is a wonderful gift of God's love, and people of contemplative reflection see so many signs of God's revealing presence. The world's extraordinary beauty, richness, healing qualities, and teaching values draw us to God. We were created for love and will be constantly unfulfilled until we are filled with love which is the ultimate reason for everything we do and are (C. 29.3). The human heart seeks meaning and fulfillment and finds them in love. God surrounds us with all kinds of invitations to love, and each of us finds that we are restless until we give ourselves to a life of love. So, God places the first invitation to love deep within our own hearts. If we do not answer this invitation to love we will never be the people we were created to be. We know God because of the love God gives to us.

Creation all around us reminds us of God's abundant love, for God has poured out a thousand graces and clothed the world with reflections of divine love. Throughout the spiritual life creation provides invitations to love. Reflecting on the wonders of creation we appreciate how it teaches us so much about life, beauty, seasons, rhythms, interdependence, and healthfulness. Creation is one of God's great invitations to love. It points us to the greatness, excellence, and generosity of God. "[O]nly the hand of God, her Beloved, was able to create this diversity and grandeur" (C. 4.3). In looking at creation we inevitably appreciate the awesomeness of God and God's overwhelming love for us. John also insists that we include men and women in appreciating God's love in creation: "Oh, then, soul, most beautiful among all creatures" (C. 1.7).

God invites us to love by means of the intense and unfulfilled longings that we experience. We feel the pain of God's absence and long for God's healing and delightful presence (C. 9.3). When John describes the profound desire of a person for the love of God he is speaking about something at the core of our humanity—an existential yearning to be who we are called to be. This desire can only be satisfied when the person "could plunge into the unfathomable spring of love" (C. 12.9). This desire is a lovesickness that has no remedy except in the pursuit of love, for "love is incurable except by things in accord with love" (C. 11.1). "The reason for this is that love of God is the soul's health, and the soul does not have full health until love is complete" (C. 11.11). Eventually, everything that is not the pursuit of love wearies a person. God has made us in such a way that we have within us the invitation to seek love, for it is only love that can bring fulfillment in life.

God draws us to love by effecting within us a distaste for all things other than God and by a self-forgetfulness achieved by the love of God (C. 1.20). John calls these actions of God in the depth of our hearts "touches" or "wounds of love." This infused love creates a passion of love and draws us to God. By these means God draws us, raises us up, detaches from creatures, and attaches us to divine life. Thus, God enkindles the will and draws the understanding. These powerful invitations to love leave us feeling that God has stolen our hearts through love (C. 9.4). The whole spiritual journey consists essentially in God drawing us to union through constant invitations to love, for "the soul drinks of the beloved's very own love that he infuses in her" (C. 26.7). God in dealing with us makes use of nothing other than love, draws us to love in everything, until we know how to do nothing else than love and walk always with the Lord in the delights of love (C. 27.8). By drawing us and infusing us with love, God makes us worthy and capable of that love (C. 32.5).

God invites us to love by teaching and leading us to love. Once the stage of beginners has passed God leads us into the depths of divine love (C. Prologue.3). God awakens love in our hearts passively in contemplation, and when we respond, God places his grace and love in us. Throughout the journey God shows us how to love God as perfectly as possible, "teaching her to love purely, freely, and disinterestedly, as he loves us, God makes her love him with the very strength with which he loves her" (C. 38.4).

We also see an invitation of God in the many gifts we have received. At this point, aware of God's awesome generosity, we feel drawn to respond. This is equally true when we see how generous

God is to others too. They and their gifts are traces of God's presence that fills us with love. We can follow these footprints that lead to God (C. 25.2-3).

God constantly invites us to union in love by the divine presence within us. This is one of the extraordinary ways in which God invites us to love. God is present to us by essence, by grace, and by spiritual affection. Reflecting on these many ways through which God is present, "the soul feels an immense hidden being from which God communicates to her some semi-clear glimpses of his divine beauty" (C. 11.4). These lead us to ardently long for what is hidden in this presence. Yet again John disrupts our way of thinking and of understanding God's role in our lives. Something happens under the transforming power of God's love that opens the way to a new vision of God and of a new transformed humanity. This includes awareness that God always remains the same but always renews all things.

John also points out to us what he calls "*an awakening of God in the soul, brought about in gentleness and love*" (F. 4.2). This awakening takes place in the center and depth of our hearts where God dwells. It is "a movement of the Word in the substance of the soul" (F. 4.4). Again, he says "this awakening is the communication of God's excellence to the substance of the soul" (F. 4.10). When John speaks about substance he refers to the most interior point within the human spirit where a person enjoys the fruits of union with God. John says God dwells in a person's heart in secret, and remains hidden in the very substance of a person's soul. Here, the power of God's love causes this awakening. It is the transformation of our vision of world reality.

Another invitation to love comes when we experience the power of the Son of God who captivates us in love. In this encounter we see everything integrated into a unified vision of God in which all creatures "disclose the beauties of their being, power, loveliness, and graces, and the root of their duration and life" (F. 4.5).

We become conscious of how all creatures find their meaning only in God, and we see the whole world in one unified vision of

God. In this vision of total harmony of the cosmos in the power and love of God, we appreciate how God moves, sustains, and governs the universe, bestowing being, power, and grace all on creatures. This awakening, this contemplative glance of reality, changes everything and we see the whole of reality as a gift of God's love.

The challenge to immerse ourselves in God's vision of love as it is presented and proclaimed by John of the Cross can seem overwhelming. However, God becomes our model. The inner life of the Trinity, where all three persons are bound together and beget, share, and intercommunicate in love, is a model of love that calls us to become part of this ongoing dynamism of love and longs to extend itself in every aspect of creation. In fact, the whole world surrounds us with God's love, and rekindles that love within us when at every turn we witness God's unending generosity and unending love. John asks us to look around and see how God's love is everywhere. This is a mystical vision of the entire creation, every aspect is part of God's gift of transforming love. Everywhere we turn we see that the world is full of God's many invitations to appreciate divine love, to welcome love into our hearts, to build our lives on this universal love.

Chapter 3
Preparing oneself for a life of love
Reflections on the Ascent of Mount Carmel

Liberating our hearts from false values

Seeking a new way of knowing God

Controlling false loves in the memory and will

Practicing detachment that leads to integration

John of the Cross often used a diagram to explain the spiritual journey. It shows Mount Carmel and all around the peak John lists the fruits of the Holy Spirit, aspects of life that they who reach the summit enjoy. There are three paths that lead into the mountain. Two of them are wide, comfortable, and seem to give easy access to the mountain top; the valley of earthly goods and the valley of heavenly goods, both of which we mistakenly think lead us to God. Some people falsely think that accumulating either material goods or spiritual goods they think lead to God is the way to growth in the spiritual life—more devotions, prayer structures, religious books, retreats, spiritual directors, and so on. This approach is an example of childish and distasteful spiritual gluttony. On John's diagram, both of these valleys are dead ends. In the center is the narrow road that leads directly to the summit, and this straight and narrow path to the summit is a journey of denial of false loves and the resulting integration of authentic love. From the top of this mountain everything looks different—the valley below, the journey, the training, oneself, the world, and God.

Introduction

We frequently speak about our spiritual development as a journey. However, it is a journey that is primarily God's work of drawing us forward, rather than our effort-filled undertaking. When left to ourselves, we seem to spend all our spiritual lives travelling without ever arriving anywhere. We remain filled with so many problems to which we do not have any answers. However, God has given us the right perspective on this journey when in Scripture we read, "I shall lead her into solitude and there speak to her heart" (Hosea 2:14). While God leads us, it is still for each of us a journey of discovery into the unknown. Every day we make an effort to go to what we do not understand.

Sometimes in our spiritual journey it seems we are running out of time, but we are not. There is lots of time. The key issue is how to use it. Answers come from all sides, and God who has the real answers for us must strain to be heard above the din of our ignorance. This journey is one of negation/integration or as John would say "nada/todo", and we need to be ready for a call we never thought we would receive. Our call is to denial not achievement, emptiness not accumulation, poverty not possessiveness, and passivity not activity. The spiritual journey implies emptying ourselves of all that is not genuine love of God so we can attain what is truly of God. An authentic spiritual journey is always through experiences of darkness and pain which we call the nights. The spiritual night is the death of all false desires, all false gods. The journey through the active nights is a purification of everything that comes through our senses, everything that comes from the outside, so that we can be renewed by the life of the Spirit within us. John describes what we can do to liberate our hearts from false loves, and how we can purify old ways of knowing, possessing, and loving God.

Liberating our hearts from false loves (The active night of the senses)

Beginners in the spiritual life are good people, often resolutely dedicated to God, whose lives are characterized by time given to prayer, fervor in religious practices, and a spirit of self-sacrifice. Their prayer is meditation. The key aspect of these people's lives is that they want to make a conscious choice to give their hearts to God. Part of this first step on the spiritual journey, the point of departure, is a willingness to actively enter the dark night of the senses (see A.1. 2.1), a period equivalent to the control of the appetites, the removal of the gratification or pleasure found in sense objects or in spiritual things that we used to think led us to God.

> One dark night,
> Fired with love's urgent longings
> --ah, the sheer grace! --
> I went out unseen,
> My house being now all stilled.

The active period of the night is a time of ascetical choice and commitment. The focus is not immediately on prayer and devotions but rather on a program of self-discipline, correction of faults, living out one's priorities, and a single-minded dedication to God. It is a deliberate undertaking to deprive ourselves of pleasures and loves that lead away from God or hinder the unified pursuit of God. It is a time when we transform and refocus our hearts' pursuits. So much of life, including the lives of dedicated people, is filled with false loves that ensnare the heart. Many people exhaust themselves pursuing objects they think will bring them love and fulfillment. False loves that are inordinate, voluntary, and habitual distort the focus of authentic love. People often misdirect the focus of their love and seek fulfillment and meaning in false loves. The active dark night of the senses is when we deprive ourselves of satisfactions in small misguided loves or when we prevent the scattering of our love among endless objects of sense. The active night of sense is a refocusing of love, a re-education of sense, a purifying of the heart, so that it is free to respond to God in authentic love.

Clinging to objects, practices, notions, experiences, and causes of religion that once helped us on our journey to God becomes an obstacle to encountering God who is not like any object of sense no matter how religious it seems. We deny objects of sense in so far as they become ends in themselves. "Only those who set aside their own knowledge and walk in God's service like unlearned children receive wisdom from God . . . . Accordingly, to reach union with the wisdom of God a person must advance by unknowing rather than by knowing" (A.1. 4.5). We realize that what we formerly knew so well will not lead us to God. When we have an inordinate attachment to an object of sense, absolutizing it, and seeing it as an end in itself, we can never give ourselves totally to God, and furthermore such attachment wearies, torments, darkens, defiles, and weakens our single-minded commitment to God (see A.1. 3.1; A.1. 4.1). "Consequently, the light of divine union cannot be established in the soul until these affections are eradicated" (A.1. 4.2). Beginners make active efforts to correct these failings—all part of a diligent preparation to give themselves more fully to God. This night is active, effort-filled on our part, but we do it only with God's help and loving support. We are active, but God is drawing us forward to union.

John gives several pieces of advice to one who wishes to actively contribute to the purification implied in the active night of sense. John seeks a re-education of sense not a putting to death of sense (mortification). He seeks a focus of the senses on God-directed values, an integration of all aspects of life in God, and not a perverted, disordered heart. He has little interest in penance for its own sake (see A.1. 3.4). John's advice is clear and practical. First, we must concentrate on bringing life in conformity with Christ's, having a greater love of Christ than anything else. The key element for entering the nights is love of Christ and desire to imitate him and to seek union that is a union of likeness in love. "First, have a habitual desire to imitate Christ in all your deeds by bringing your life in conformity with his" (A.1. 13.3). We cannot focus on love of God when our hearts are focused on many other objects. Second, we need to renounce any sensory satisfaction that is not exclusively for the honor and glory of God or not integrated into a God-directed life. Third, we must bring the four natural passions in harmony and peace by choosing to do that which is most difficult, the removal of habitual, voluntary imperfections that lead one away from God. Fourth, we view ourselves honestly in light of our failings and are ready to hear from others of failings of which we are unaware. In addition to these concrete recommendations, John advises readers to put into practice the suggestions he gave on the sketch of Mount Carmel that can be summed up in his first proposal, "always choose that which is most difficult." In spiritual life we must make tough decisions. Although John, with his typical realism and concern, says "well, endeavor to do these things." John approaches the purification of the night of sense with his usual sense of balance and appreciation of human responsiveness. "[T]he appetites are not all equally detrimental, nor are all equally a hindrance to the soul . . . . to mortify them entirely is impossible in this life. . . they are not such a hindrance as to prevent one from attaining divine union" (A.1. 11.2).

John's advice for today in approaching the active night of sense could possibly be: imitate Christ in the daily decisions of life; practice moderation in the exercise of external senses, and avoid excesses of novelty, new sensations and experiences. Without personal display and without inconveniencing others, we should be suspicious of the easy and comfortable, seek what is the most difficult especially regarding charity to others, always choose what is the most loving thing to do, and control pride in all its manifestations. The active night of sense is really a re-education of the senses, a strengthening of sense in its correct use in all external activities and actions. Thus, we monitor touch, taste, looking, words, body, and activity of passions. It is God's way of preparing a person for the life of the Spirit.

Reflections on the text

God calls many to make this journey and gives them the grace for advancing. If we choose to journey to the top of Mount Carmel we must pass through a dark night on the way to union with God in love. The trials we must face on this climb are numerous, intense, and even beyond our understanding. However, we must acknowledge that many who begin this journey do not complete it because they do not want to face the pain and darkness it entails, or because they just do not understand what is happening to them, or because they have no suitable guide to help them. If we desire to make this climb and are ready to make the effort, then God will help us. Unfortunately, many of us make little progress because we never break away from the methods of beginners. Some of us, instead of abandoning ourselves to God and cooperating with divine grace, block such help by inappropriate action or by resistance to grace. We will need to leave aside the satisfaction that comes with primitive devotions and accept the aridity of this transition. God works in us, purifying our former ways of spiritual life.

We can only undertake this exodus when motivated by love of God. In our spiritual journey we must pass through two dark experiences or nights—one is the purgation of the senses—an experience of beginners, and the other of spirit—an experience of proficients. The first part of this night is the loss or denial and purification of all sensible appetites for external things that we think lead us to God. We must control these before moving on. We cannot enter this night of our own initiative. We have a part to play, but God is drawing us forward. It is a grace when God places one in this night. This first night is the lot of beginners as God introduces them into the state of contemplation. Journeying through the nights is a shortcut to growth in the spiritual life.

Our journey is a night because it involves painful deprivation which is like a night to our senses. It is a night for our intellect which will need to leave aside knowledge that comes through the senses to emphasize faith. It is a night because the end of our journey is God who is clouded in darkness for us while we remain in this life. There are three parts of one developing night that moves from early evening when things fade out of sight (deprivation), to the total darkness of midnight (faith), then on to the early dawn and a new rising (encountering God). We must purify our hearts from all false affections and attachments. We learn to know God in faith and not through intellectual information. God communicates to us in the night of contemplation.

We must control any attachments and false loves that take the place of God. The spiritual journey to union in love leads us to the best situation possible for us in life and leads us to become our best and true selves. However, it begins with the challenge to purify all experiences that come through our senses. The gratifications that come through senses hinder us from getting to know God, and we must deny our appetites for these false values and goals. When John uses the term "appetites" he means self-indulgent, voluntary attachments, affections, or desires for creatures as habitual ends in themselves. We do not seek to destroy our senses and faculties, but to re-direct, re-educate, and refocus them on God and divine values. However, when we deny our appetites their normal objects, there remains a void within us which is a darkness in our lives until it is replaced with the love of God.

We remain incapable of enlightenment until all appetites and false desires are purified. Attachment to creatures as ends in themselves cannot coexist with the illumination that comes from

God alone. No one can serve two masters. This extends to all human knowledge which is ignorance in comparison to the wisdom of God. To journey towards God we must walk away from all that is not God. We must learn not to make a big deal of ourselves or of things. If we identify with creatures we become like them. If we identify with God we draw near to union. The spiritual journey is a journey away from slavery to false values and false loves that control our liberty of spirit.

This night of sense consists in the purification of all disordered, habitual, voluntary appetites that crave inappropriate sensory satisfaction. We find in spiritual life that giving free rein to appetites—deliberate attachment to creatures in place of God—causes us harm in two ways; it deprives us of the ability to recognize God's spirit and it wearies, weakens, and torments us in our daily lives and in the pursuit of God. Uncontrolled appetites with their false loves torment us, and instead of us controlling them we are controlled by them. Love of God and exclusive attachments to creatures cannot coexist. We seek self-control of those habitual, voluntary appetites that impede union with God. Attachment to anything finite never satisfies our infinite longings in life, whereas the Spirit of God brings fullness. When we give free rein to appetites we are always dissatisfied and bitter, and hungry for more. If we do not refrain from disordered appetites they end up controlling and tormenting us. "Appetite" comes from the word "to desire" and refers to all the false desires that lead us away from God.

We enter the night of the senses in two ways. First, with God's grace we actively contribute with our own efforts. Second, God accomplishes the work in us, and we are passive recipients. (John deals with this second in the book of the *Dark Night*). *Regarding our active involvement we should do the following.* 1. Have a habitual desire to get to know Christ and to imitate him in all we do. 2. Renounce all sensory satisfactions, develop indifference to gratification, and stress only the will of God. 3. Control and purify the four passions—joy, hope, fear, and sorrow, by always being ready to make the difficult life-changing decisions. 4. Intensify self-knowledge with awareness of our emptiness before God; have a habit of mind to question and be suspicious of our motives, biases, and needs.

To journey through the nights we need courage and constancy and these qualities will be supported by intense love. John of the Cross was convinced that if we embrace these commitments earnestly and put them into practice they will lead to significant benefits. The longing of love for union with the Lord enables us to confront the appetites and control and deny any satisfaction that does not lead to God. Our desire for union is what motivates us. We must have a greater love for Christ than for anything else. Love will be the motivation for all further stages in this exciting journey. "O great God of love, and Lord. How many riches do you place in the soul that neither loves nor is satisfied except in you alone, for you give yourself to it and become one with it through love" (L. 11).

The active night of sense is the first step in a movement towards an intense, well-focused love, centered on God who is the ultimate goal of human existence. There begins a sense of joy in being liberated from captivity to senses, passions, and appetites. The first part of the journey involves denial and purification. Only when the appetites no longer war against the spirit can we experience the peace of early encounters with the Lord. The journey through the nights is full of darkness and suffering but once made a person looks back with joy.

Seeking a new way of knowing God (Active night of the spirit—especially the intellect)

It is easy to think we are burdened in our journey to God by pleasures and satisfactions of sense. But we are also burdened by what we know, what we remember, and what we love, and also by how we know, remember, and love. These spiritual faculties (intellect-knowing, memory-possessing, will-affective power or desiring) must be purified if we are to journey to union with God in love. We might think we know who God is, but we do not, and our false images and knowledge must be purified by faith. We might remember how good God has been to us and use this as a point of departure for our journey, but this is so limiting it destroys who God can be for us—something we can only grasp through a purification by hope. We might even strive to love God in our own way, with enthusiasm and dedication, but we thus make God in our own image and likeness, and we have to find a new way of loving which only comes through the purification of charity. This part of purification consists in our deliberate efforts to clarify knowledge, memory, love, and desire.

The active night of spirit refers to a process of purification of any satisfaction that comes from the spiritual faculties. It means purifying the intellect in faith, the memory in hope, and the will in charity. "Faith causes darkness and a void in understanding in the intellect, hope begets an emptiness of possessions in the memory, and charity produces the nakedness and emptiness of affection and joy in all that is not God" (A.2. 6.2). John deals with the active night of the spirit in faith in Book II of the *Ascent*, and the active night of the spirit in hope and love in Book III. Accompanying this purification of the spirit by means of the three theological virtues is the move away from meditation and discursive prayer to the preliminaries of recollection for contemplation where an individual lives with a quiet, loving attention to God, abandoning the imagination. When a person can no longer meditate, finds no satisfaction in using his or her imagination, and enjoys remaining alone in loving awareness of God, such a person is ready to move on (see A.2. 13).

Book II of the *Ascent* deals with the night of faith which John sees as the nerve of the spiritual life. "Only by means of faith, in divine light exceeding all understanding, does God manifest himself to the soul. The greater one's faith the closer is one's union with God" (A.2. 9.1). In speaking of faith, John refers both to the mystery and its content (see A.2. 2-3) and to a person's attitudes in accepting faith (see A.2. 4) which is itself a part of the mystery.

Faith is a personal acceptance of a personal God. The images we have of God are very important for the whole development of the spiritual life. In fact, the active night of the spirit consists in purifying one's images of God. No natural knowledge can ever be a proximate means of union with God, because it can never conceive him as he is (A.1. 4.7).

Reflections on the text

Book two of the *Ascent* describes the active night of spirit which consists in the purification or *divesting the spirit of all its imperfections and appetites for spiritual possessions*. This is a more intense and painful experience than the night of sense. We are dealing with the purification of the intellect in faith. When the intellect no longer focuses on its own natural objects of knowledge and information it finds itself in painful darkness and emptiness until illumined by faith.

> In darkness and secure,
> By the secret ladder, disguised,
> --ah, the sheer grace!—
> In darkness and concealment,
> my house being now all stilled.

The dark night of spirit is darker and more interior because it deprives the rational, superior part of light and understanding. Our knowledge is generally acquired through the intellect, but not the knowledge that faith gives. However, faith brings darkness not because of the absence of light but because of the overwhelming brightness and illumination of a new knowledge of God. Faith is obscure for us because it deals with divinely revealed truths which transcend human understanding. The brightness of revealed truths overwhelms and blinds us. Faith informs us of matters we have never seen or known. It is beyond all natural knowledge. The night of faith becomes our guide. The dark night is our only light. Faith blinds us to all false knowledge of God as it leads us to illumination.

We need to be in darkness in order to be guided by faith. This darkness not only regards the sense part of a person but also that part which relates to God and to spiritual things, so the rational and higher part of human nature. After all, we seek a supernatural encounter—so beyond the natural. This means voluntarily emptying ourselves of any affection or desire for earthly or heavenly goods. Moreover, this active night of spirit refers to what we can achieve through our own efforts. We can contribute stillness, means of inspiration, attentiveness, concentration, silence, active presence, and so on. Then we actively avoid former consoling devotions, exclusiveness to people, and practices that formerly made up our spirituality. We must stop relying on anything that we can understand, taste, feel, or imagine. Faith is beyond all this understanding, tasting, feeling, and imagining. Only when we are blind and empty and in darkness can we allow God to guide us. We must not rely on any knowledge or experience that we have of God since this blocks true knowledge and God-given experience. However impressive our knowledge or feeling for God is, it has no resemblance to God.

God will communicate divine life and union to those who are more conformed to God's will. This supernatural union is not based on our understanding or feeling, but only on the purity and exclusive focus of our love of God. Sometimes we lack conformity of our will with God's, either in the case of a specific action or because of an established habit. We cannot achieve union of wills until everything contrary to this conformity or union of likeness is rejected. Only when we deprive ourselves of all that is not God can we be illumined by and transformed in God. Perfect transformation is only possible with perfect purity.

The union with God is achieved by purifying our intellect, memory, and will by means of the theological virtues of faith, hope, and charity. The three theological virtues cause darkness and emptiness in the spiritual faculties by depriving them of their natural objects. Faith affirms what cannot be understood by the intellect, hope rejects memories and stresses what is unpossessed in the future, and charity abandons all other loves to love God alone. This leads to the transformation we seek. "The soul is not united with God in this life through understanding, or through enjoyment, or through imagination, or through any other sense; but only faith, hope, and charity (according to the intellect, memory, and will) can unite the soul with God in this life" (A.2. 6.1). The intellect must be perfected in the darkness of faith, the memory in the emptiness of hope, and the will in the absence of every affection. This is the active night of spirit because we do what lies within our power to enter this night. The whole spiritual journey can be understood as the transformation of the spiritual faculties by the three theological virtues. This is the darkness that leads to illumination. We must discover these new ways of knowing, possessing, and loving God.

We journey to union with God by means of a narrow path. In this journey *we restrict, or narrow, the focus of our spiritual faculties so that they focus on God alone*. Few people are willing to accept the pains of this narrow path, and so few find their way to God. So many people dabble in all kinds of methods that they hope will lead to God. They utilize all sorts of devotions and get nowhere. When the narrow path arrives as the summit of Mount Carmel it opens to the wonders of God's graces and love. Few people have the knowledge, preparation, and desire to commit themselves to emptying the spirit of false values. The journey to God is along a narrow path that climbs high on Mount Carmel. Many people are too burdened with false possessions to make the trip. Some people will try any and every method to lead to God, dabbling in all kinds of petty practices. They do this rather than accept the narrow path that alone leads to God. Many people seek themselves and their satisfactions in the pursuit of God.

Nothing created or imagined can serve the intellect as a means for union with God. In fact, attachment to what is grasped by the intellect is an obstacle to union. Rather, we know God in contemplation which is a passive gift of God, a secret wisdom beyond the intellect's ability. In this experience the intellect is blind and a person walks in faith. We do not earn or achieve knowledge of God. It is a gift in contemplation and we receive it passively. Everything the intellect can understand, the will experience, and the imagination can picture is completely unlike God. Nothing in this world resembles God. So, we cannot know God by anything this world offers. We need the active nights of sense and spirit to purify all sensory and spiritual knowledge of God.

So, *we must purify those sources of knowledge that really do not help us in our journey to God*. Some originate naturally through the senses and we purify these in the active night of sense. Supernatural knowledge which comes to the intellect through the senses must be purified through the night of spirit. These sources are not reliable as sources for true knowledge or divine communications. They cannot serve as a means for union since they have no proportionate relationship to God. We must also divest ourselves of anything that comes through the imagination or phantasy—because discursive interior senses cannot teach us anything beyond what is perceived through the senses. We must instead abide in calm restfulness where God can fill us with peace and refreshment. Supernatural knowledge can diminish faith, impede the Spirit, be sought for the satisfaction it gives, can reduce fervor and God's favors, and open the door to evil. Spiritual knowledge that comes through the senses is not reliable and can easily deceive the person in his or her spiritual journey. Supernatural knowledge that comes through the senses includes visions, images, heard communications, and sensitive feelings of delight.

Part of the process of moving to a *new way of knowing God is the transition from discursive meditation to contemplation*. There are three signs that indicate it is appropriate for us to discontinue discursive meditation. 1. We realize we can no longer mediate as we used to with the satisfaction we used to receive from our prayer. 2. We have no desire to apply our imagination to rekindle our prayer, and this used to be the answer when meditation became more difficult. 3. We prefer to remain alone in a loving attention towards God without acts and exercises that we formerly used. When these three signs are present at the same time, then we must remain in peace and follow the lead of the Holy Spirit. This transition is not easy since we are leaving something we knew well and were successful at it and moving to an unknown.

John of the Cross was very concerned that we not be misled by spiritual communications that we believe come through visions. The night of spirit purifies desires for special divine interventions, visions, and supernatural communications. Seeking God's spiritual interventions in life is not a good thing to do. There are boundaries between this world and the next, and we should not seek to transcend them. The desire for knowledge of things through supernatural means is worse than seeking satisfaction and gratification through sensitive means. John reminds us, "Only by means of faith, in divine light exceeding all understanding, does God manifest Himself to the soul" (A.2 9.1).

Controlling false loves in the memory and will (Active night of the spirit—memory and will)

Book III of the *Ascent* deals with the active night of the spirit as a process whereby with God's help we purify the memory of false images of God—and all its images, even our most enthusiastic and satisfying, are false because they all fall short of who God can be for us in our hope. Much of our image of God comes from the accumulation of all our good memories of God's interventions in our lives. Memories are discursive and we need a new kind of insight into God. One of the results of union with God is "forgetfulness of all things, since forms and knowledge are gradually being erased from the memory" (A.3. 2.8). Consequently, "God now possesses the faculties as their complete lord, because of their transformation in him. And consequently it is he who divinely moves and commands them according to his divine spirit and will" (A.3. 2.8). As we let go and detach from memory we enjoy tranquility and peace, and gain freedom from temptations that can come through the memory. The less other objects are possessed by the memory, the more we can possess God in hope. We do not love the God of our memories but the God of our hope.

Book III of the *Ascent* goes on to deal with the rebirth of love through the active night of spirit. The task here is to change some of what we love or are addicted to and how we love, so that the full force of love can be directed to all that is of God (see Deut 6:5). This implies purifying the will (affectivity) from inordinate attachments, those voluntary, habitual imperfections that diminish a single-minded and single-hearted pursuit of the love of God. Loving union is achieved through the will, so one must desire nothing that is alien to God. Here John uses the unusual word "appetites" by which he means generally a tendency to show affection for anything that leads away from God. John is very detailed in listing every kind of appetite or obstacle whether temporal, natural, sensual, moral, supernatural, or spiritual. John seeks a life of total self-surrender in love. "To come to enjoy what you have not you must go by a way where you enjoy not" (A.1. 13.11); and again, "Deny your desires and you will find what your heart longs for" (S. 15). This is the work of bringing one's will and affectivity in conformity with God's will and love. The will is not just the act of choice and will power, but what motivates desire and governs choice.

Reflections on the text

Book I of the *Ascent* dealt with the active night of the senses, Book II with the active night of the spirit, the purification of the intellect in faith. *Book III deals with the purification of the other two spiritual faculties: the active night of the memory in hope, and of the will in charity.* Since the three spiritual faculties depend on each other, the purification of the intellect in faith will simultaneously impact the other two spiritual faculties. However, we must also actively and deliberately purify our memory of its false ways of possessing God, and our will of its false ways of loving God or of diverting our love to objects away from God. Let us remind ourselves that we are dealing with the active night of spirit and consequently with our own contributions to this process of purification. The active night of spirit consists in our efforts to purify the spiritual faculties of their false or limited contents and methods of knowing, possessing, and loving God.

God is our teacher and guide. So, as with the intellect, we must deprive the memory and will of their natural objects so they can receive an inflow and illumination from God. In the case of the memory we must empty it of all former images so that it is not attached to any earthly or spiritual object. We appreciate God's loving compassion towards us less with memories than with hope. The memory can only be absorbed in hope of God when it lives in forgetfulness of past images and lives without remembrance of anything. We should not store up in the memory objects from the five senses but leave them aside and forget them. The memory cannot be united to God and at the same time be united to forms and images that are not God, for God has no form or image comprehensible to the memory. This purification does not lead to the destruction of the memory but to its perfection in hope.

There are *three kinds of harm that arise when we do not purify the memory.* The first harm comes from the world around us, in so far as relying exclusively on the memory leads to falsehoods, imperfections, appetites, judgments, loss of time, and so on. The second harm resulting from a misdirected focus on the memory comes from evils and delusions that result from false images. The third harm is that memories become impediments to moral and spiritual goods, as we become disturbed by memories and unable to focus on the incomprehensible God.

When we control the negative effects of memories *we find three opposite benefits that result from forgetfulness.* Instead of the disturbances derived from ideas in the memory we enjoy peace of soul and purity of conscience. Instead of the temptations from evil we find freedom in our thoughts and ideas. Instead of the blocks to moral and spiritual development we discover recollection and forgetfulness and we become disposed to the guidance of the Holy Spirit. Worrying about memories can never remedy the disturbance we feel but only produce further distress. As we try to endure all things with tranquility and peace, so we should respond in this way to memories. We should seek tranquility of soul and peace in all things both in times of adversity or prosperity. Memories make us look back, whereas we should be looking ahead in hope.

The active night of the spirit includes the purification of the will in charity. This means we must purify the will so that we can employ all faculties, appetites, operations, and emotions towards union with God. The will controls appetites, faculties, and passions, directing them to God in love. There are four passions that direct our lives to God or, when inordinate, away from God. These four passions—joy, hope, sorrow, and fear—must focus all we do on following the will of God and integrating all we do in union with God. We must work to purify each one individually, aware that all four are intimately connected and wax or wane together. John urges us to avoid dividing our will among many objects but to unite it in one single ability and strength directed to God.

Joy is the passion and emotion of the will that results from the satisfaction we find in an object we seek. This joy is active, which means we can seek it or not. However, we should only find joy in those things that lead us to God. *What we should not do is seek or find joy in objects that lead us away from God*. There are many aspects of daily life—God's gifts—that bring us joy, and we can make all these part of our integrated commitment to God. We can find joy in objects that lead us to God or in those that lead us away from God. We must choose only the former. John divides the possible objects of joy into six groups: temporal, natural, sensory, moral, supernatural, and spiritual. All aspects of our daily lives can be integrated in our total commitment, and we can find joy in many ways that are part of our unified God-directed lives.

When we allow ourselves to find joy in creatures as ends in themselves we blunt our dedication to the joy of union with God. We fail when we seek joy in temporal goods such as wealth, status, family, and so on, making them ends in themselves. All these are good in themselves, especially when used in the service of God. However, often we can become attached to them and misdirect our joy to them instead of to God. If we free our hearts from joy in exclusively pursuing satisfaction in temporal goods many blessings result, including freedom of spirit, clarity of judgment, liberality, peace, and purity of spiritual commitment. Temporal goods are God's gifts and therefore we direct our gratitude to the goodness of God and use these gifts well. When we find joy and satisfaction exclusively in temporal goods we become forgetful of God. Focusing our joy on creatures as the exclusive object of satisfaction weakens our judgment, diminishes our spiritual commitment, and results in lukewarmness to spiritual values. When we do this, we become more committed to creatures than to God. When we detach ourselves from making temporal goods ends in themselves we end up with a new appreciation for them.

Practicing detachment that leads to integration

One of the major developments in the last couple of decades has been an extraordinary interest in integrating faith with daily life and activity. Spirituality permeates our commitment to every aspect of life. This results when we realize that all life including our family and working lives with their new focuses of call are always a re-living of the baptismal challenge to belong to Christ, to live and love for him. This leads us to relate differently to self, to others, and even to the cosmos because of a new way of living our relationship to Jesus. The service of others in daily life is a particularly splendid way of realizing this. This call will need to be renewed on a daily basis, as we face increasing demands that must never lead to a reduced ideal of our calling. Both feeling called by faith and yearning for personal integration, we as Christians strive to respond each day to the implications of that call we feel deep in our hearts.

John tells us that there are two qualities necessary for the spiritual journey, poverty and nakedness. Again, we must interpret these dynamically and not statically. The journey consists in us striving every day to become poor in spirit, and endeavoring each day to strip ourselves of any false values that lead us away from God. John considers that we are inauthentic when we accumulate goods—material or spiritual, and find satisfaction in their possession. Let us keep in mind that authenticity is not achieved by accumulation, by adding on more qualities—as if the symptom of our disorder is hunger. Rather, authenticity is found in the depth of each of us in that zone of divine life that God has placed in each of us. The problem is that our lives are cluttered with too many false values that block our progress. We are not primarily hungry for spiritual life; rather we have indigestion from too much artificiality, false values, and greed for a merely sensual life. We must attain poverty and nakedness on all levels, not only material, but moral, spiritual, and religious as well.

Growth in the spiritual life is primarily God's work within us, we do not earn advancement, but we are being drawn forward by God, even in the active phases. For our part we must desire to succeed in this journey; we must really want it more than anything else. Many say they do, but their half-hearted commitment shows clearly it is not a priority for them. We can show our desire by getting rid of any obstacles that hinder progress in the journey. This will include self-discipline, correction of faults, establishing priorities, removal of gratification in anything that leads away from God. We must also cultivate a healthy image of God by finding new ways to know, remember, and love God. While contemplation is God's gift, we can contribute by creating a suitable environment in which prayer can develop. We need to become comfortable in solitude and meditation, seek genuine freedom of spirit, and appreciate beauty, joy, and enthusiasm.

Reflections on the text

So, the active night of spirit is a process of purification of the spiritual faculties of intellect, memory, and will. It is above all an effort to pursue simplicity and to prepare for receptivity. It is active but non-discursive—active in the exercise of faith, in maintaining oneself at rest, in stillness, in being present to God, in being attentive, in discerning carefully, in concentrating, in receiving loving knowledge (see A.2. 12-14). It is also active in deliberately refraining from pursuing only sensible satisfaction, in accepting grace, in freedom, in perseverance, and in patience (see N.1. 10).

Nowadays, these appetites that hinder union are just as likely to be collective as personal, and justified as criteria and convictions rather than seen as clear failures. Thus, burnout, keeping institutions going, sexual dominance by males, corruption at all levels of society, lack of women's equality and roles in society, inadequate commitment to social justice, claims to maintain purity of doctrine, are some of the appetites that take people's energy away from love of Christ, but are justified and religiously supported. Likewise, people can love their virtues, good habits, graces, talents, motivations, dedication, projects and causes, religious observances, ceremonies and outward liturgical forms, one's spiritual director—all notable spiritual values that can lead to or away from union with God in love (see A.3. 33-40).

We must continue to purify our image of God. John's warnings against visions, apparitions, private revelations, inadequate discernment by both spiritual director and directee, are equally present today, as religious people get caught up in their favorite devotions, causes, approaches to Church teachings, chosen leaders, media personalities, and gurus. All these attachments must be recognized and put in order.

For John detachment means integration. John's approach is to pursue denial and at first sight his is a spirituality of negation in dark nights. However, John's denial is never exclusively negative. In fact, when he talks about detachment in its many forms he is using the language and concepts of his day. He is very positive towards God's gifts of this world and humanity's basic qualities and reactions. What he is against is the absolutizing of possessiveness. When he speaks of detachment, denial of appetites, sacrifice, and so on, he refers to failures to focus life on God alone—anything that distracts or leads us to lose focus on God. The active nights of sense and spirit call us to purify anything that leads us away from an integrated pursuit of God. Absolutizing detachment or a spirit of sacrifice or a life of negation would simply mean we are turning a religious practice into an end in itself. We must love God with every aspect of our lives; everything must be integrated into a single-minded and single-hearted pursuit of God. The *Ascent of Mount Carmel* calls for a spirituality of integration of love.

The seeking of spiritual growth is a special gift of God, a gift from on high that must not be contaminated by the corruptions of this world's systems and values. This must be our overwhelming desire and focus, filling our hearts and leaving no room for anything else. Always we need to remain empty of all other desires so as to be filled with God alone. Our journey needs to be in sacrifice, patience, silence, and self-denial, so as to enjoy the inner resurrection of the Spirit. In silence, prayer, service, and work we will find strength of spirit, and in solitude and forgetfulness of all that does not lead us to God, we can pursue the deepening of our commitment. In all this we have a role to play—the active night of senses and of spirit. Christian tradition has always insisted that every Christian must actively seek to remove sinful tendencies from life in order to prepare self for life with God. It is a constant of tradition that we must acknowledge our own sinfulness and undergo conversion before we can begin the journey to God. We know that transformation is God's work within us, but we must ready ourselves for this gift by the removal of sin and the development of virtue. Nowadays we do not think much about asceticism but it is an essential part of our preparation for a life of love. Many people think John presents a program of mortification, putting to death all desires, passions, and faculties. This is far from the truth. He urges us to redirect or reeducate every aspect of our lives and focus everything on God. We must purify false loves before we can give ourselves to authentic love. Once totally empty of false values, a person can be filled with God and discover a new set of values, feelings, and practices that lead to the life we seek.

Chapter 4
Feeling the thrill and excitement of the journey of love

Reflections on the Spiritual Canticle

A period of preparation for love (stanzas 1-5)

Longing for clearer knowledge of the Beloved (stanzas 6-12)

The unitive stage—part I; spiritual betrothal (stanzas 13-21)

The unitive stage part II; spiritual marriage (stanzas 22-40)

> Total union in spiritual marriage (stanzas 22-35)
>
> Longing for perfect union in glory (stanzas 36-40)

The *Spiritual Canticle* is an extraordinary poem and commentary, filled with the thrill, excitement, and longing of two lovers. At times it is fast-paced, moving with impatient love and longing, and at other times it is slow-paced, as the two lovers spend time enjoying each other's company. John started the poem in prison in Toledo, and there are indications that this is John's own journey of love (see C. 27.8; 28.8; 36.4). The poem begins with the lover's cry of pain at perceived abandonment by her Beloved. "Why have you left me? Where have you hidden, my love? Why did you leave so soon after filling me with your love?" The first five verses describe painful purification in the lover's yearnings and search. "Tell him I love so much that I am sick, I suffer, and I feel near death without him." With verse six the scene changes from purification to illumination in contemplation. "This love-sickness I feel cannot be healed except by your presence, my love." Spiritual betrothal starts with verse twelve, but the bride-to-be barely gets chance to yearn for deeper union before the bridegroom urges her to go back to further purification, telling her she is not ready for the union for which she longs. With verse twenty-two the period of spiritual marriage begins, "The bride has entered the sweet garden of her desire." And from verse thirty-six we read of the final period of intense longing for full union in eternity. "Let us rejoice, my love, and go forward to behold ourselves in your beauty."

John of the Cross is unquestionably the mystical doctor of divine and human love, and nowhere do we see this better than in the *Spiritual Canticle* which treats of the entire spiritual life exclusively from an affective perspective. It shows us the growth of love from early anxieties and yearnings to God's illuminative guidance and teachings on love, and on to the in-breaking of God's love into the searching soul. It then proclaims the intensity of union between the lovers in mutual peace, surrender, and self-gift, and then speaks of the Lover's gift of equality in love.

Introduction

John tells us that the *Spiritual Canticle* deals with the whole of the spiritual journey from one's early service of God to the final stage of spiritual development (often referred to as spiritual marriage) (see SC. Theme.1-2). The *Spiritual Canticle* presents a series of steps in a growing relationship of love between a future bride—the lover and the Beloved—God. It describes a process from a heart that is enslaved to false values and false ways of loving, to a liberated heart that centers all on God, integrates all good aspects of life into God's will, and has learnt how to love as God wishes.

As in his other works, John follows the traditional view of the spiritual life as divided into the purgative way of beginners (C. 1-5), the illuminative way of the proficient (C. 6-12), and the unitive way of the perfect (C. 13-40). The latter stage is divided into the two phases of union, namely spiritual engagement (C. 13-21) and spiritual marriage (C. 22-40). The focal point of the journey is always love, and even in the early stages of preparation we are always dealing with the deep yearnings of a lover: "Where have you hidden Beloved"; and with one who already knows the Beloved; "Him I love most, tell him I am sick, I suffer, and I die." John writes his poem to portray the dynamic attitudes of one who pursues deeper love. Thus, the two parts of preparation (C. 1-5 and C. 6-12) encourage a sense of urgency in the reader. In the original Spanish, there are no adjectives or adverbs in these sections, and both the poem and its teachings move urgently and rapidly to union. However, once he arrives at the two stages of union he urges the reader to savor the experience, and so he fills the stanzas with a cascade of adjectives and adverbs to describe the fullness and richness of the experience.

A period of preparation for love (Stanzas 1-5)

The poem describes the relationship between two lovers. It begins with the future bride's cry of pain at feeling abandoned by her Beloved. She asks for help in finding him and tells the world of her fearless determination to discover where he is. The only response she gets is from creation that tells her he has passed by and left something of his own beauty in its midst for her to recognize. This is an extraordinary beginning of the love poem, and the depth of the future bride's love is evident from the first line. So, like the lover, each person begins this journey with an awareness of the meaning of life in the context of eternity (C. 1.1) and a profound longing for God, as he or she anxiously searches for a relationship of loving union (C. 1.2). While the *Ascent* and the *Dark Night* begin with privation, the *Spiritual Canticle* begins with painful and unfulfilled longing, and then love leads the person seeking God to want to be deprived of all that is not love of God in order to focus on love alone. "[The soul] longs for union with him through clear and essential vision. She records her longings of love and complains to him of his felt absence, especially since his love wounds her" (C. 1.2).

This is a stage where the lover wishes to leave aside everything that hinders the development of love, and this includes leaving aside previous false images of God (C. 1.3-4, 8). God inspires this enthusiasm for the search, and one soon discovers that this is a journey of transformation—a mature spiritual journey of purification of inadequate expressions of love and the development of strong love. This journey starts with a deeper self-understanding and a sense of profound gratitude, as the lover receives the initial revelations of God and becomes more aware of the pervasive presence of God. This initial phase of the journey is an ongoing purification, as the lover experiences sorrow, abandonment, spiritual dryness, and unfulfilled longing at the frequent absences of the Beloved. He or she learns to seek faith without understanding or satisfactions and in complete detachment from all that is not God. This is a time of pain and self-forgetfulness, as the lover rejects all objects of sense, experiences the purifying effects of divine communications, and just feels sick with longing for enriching love.

The development of love is only possible in a heart that is free and that has overcome all attachments to creatures as ends in themselves and controlled the three great enemies of personal growth—the world and its false values, evil that surrounds us, and human weakness (see C. stanza 3, also "The Precautions"). A person discovers that God is within his or her heart but hidden, and to find God one must leave aside every other interest that is in opposition to God or not part of one's integrated commitment to God. This includes all former knowledge, understanding, activities of the faculties of intellect, memory, and will, as well as self-centered satisfactions. In this period a person also fosters an awareness of his or her failures and sense of emptiness without God, cultivates a longing for God, and seeks God in faith, love, and unknowing.

These are not the struggles of a seeker but those of a lover. The lover must be aware that God is not like any understandings or experiences one may have of God, and that God does not act as one expects. "It is noteworthy that, however elevated God's communications and the experiences of his presence are, and however sublime a person's knowledge of him may be, these are not God essentially, nor are they comparable to him because, indeed, he is still hidden to the soul" (C. 1.3). This is where the Beloved's absences and withdrawals purify one's love (C. 1.16). A person should rejoice in the discoveries he or she makes, maintain a sense of urgency in the search, and center everything on love. Here, God is the primary actor, drawing us to divine life. God visits us and thus raises us up, and then withdraws and leaves us in painful longings of love (C. 1.22).

Since direct contact with God is not possible for human beings in this life, one can use intermediaries both to learn about God and to communicate with God. One's desires, affections, longings, and willingness to suffer for love act like messengers to

God, letting God know how much a person longs for divine union, and God welcomes these signs of love (C. 2.1). The person finds that the faculties of intellect, memory, and will no longer help, and he or she experiences an inability in knowing God (C. 2.6). But, the lover learns that these intermediaries are insufficient. One must undertake a single-minded pursuit of God that has two stages: first, one must move away from self-centeredness and all hindrances that are not God; second, one needs to undertake the practice of virtues and enter into assiduous contemplative prayer, and do both these with courageous perseverance (C. 3.1).

Leaving aside everything that leads away from God, the lover begins to see more and more how all creation reveals the wonders of God's love, and so he or she carefully reads the book of creation for signs of the Beloved. "This reflection on creatures, this observing that they are things made by the hand of God, her Beloved, strongly awakens the soul to love him" (C. 4.3). One appreciates the grandeur and abundance of God's love in creation. A person can see traces of God's presence in the world and deepen his or her understanding of the mysteries of the Incarnation by which the Son clothed the world in beauty (C. 5.1). This is very different than the experience of the dark night, but it is painful, for although there is some knowledge gained in this experience, it is insufficient and brings little satisfaction, and so one's inner spirit seems torn apart, and one feels abandoned, even rejected. This is a time of early purification of love and the first steps in discovering new ways of knowing and loving.

Reflections on the text

A relationship with God based on knowledge and love is the essential and distinguishing characteristic and purpose of Christianity. Many good Christians, including ourselves, who understand this, want to know and love God more. We might enthusiastically learn bits and pieces of information about God and accumulate gestures of love as signs of our dedication. As we accumulate small acts of love amidst our busy and multi-focused lives, a small number of the more dedicated among us begin to realize that constantly adding more small signs of love is good but insufficient. A time must come when we make a deliberate choice to focus our entire lives on the pursuit of the knowledge and love of God. We do not abandon any of the positive, fulfilling, and life-giving aspects of human existence, but integrate all of life in one great fundamental dedication to the will and values of God.

Once we make this choice—that all life must center on God— then everything else changes. Instead of prior casual encounters with God, we now want to know as much as possible about God and learn how to better respond to God in loving dedication and in the pursuit of God's will. Looking back over what maybe has been a good life, we sense how inadequate it was and even feel guilty at seeing such partial, mediocre dedication. Now, we feel unworthy, long for a deeper relationship, and experience pain at seeing our inadequate love. As dedicated people we then turn to God and cry out:

> Where have you hidden,
> Beloved, and left me moaning?
> you fled like the stag
> after wounding me;
> I went out calling you, but you were gone.

At this point in our journey we will want to know and love God more, and *will feel God is hiding and is unwilling to reveal the divine self to us*. Like a stag, God seems to be present then swiftly departs, leaving us enthused but feeling abandoned. We must learn that in this life God always remains more hidden than revealed. No matter the extent of our new-found dedication, God always remains hidden from us in this life, and the knowledge we gain and the love we show are always partial. Even at this early stage we must realize that God is not "out there" in all kinds of new experiences and gleanings of information—none of these reveal God to us. Rather, God is hiding in the innermost part of our hearts, and discovering

God there is the key way to experience God's love and uncover the secret mystery of our faith.

Once we decide to center our lives totally on God, *we will want to integrate every aspect of life in that vision and leave nothing out.* This is not easy, especially since God does not seem as responsive as we expect, and pain, sorrow, and a sense of God's absences seem to be common when we expect God to be as visibly enthusiastic as we feel. Nevertheless, we need to rejoice in what we do not know and understand about God rather than in what we think we know. From the start of this journey to deeper knowledge and love, we must grasp the reality that God is not like we think God is and God does not act as we thought God might.

In this early, enthusiastic stage of our journey to deeper knowledge and love of God we *naturally want God to know the depth of our love* and want messengers to tell God of this love. So we announce:

> Shepherds, you who go
> up through the sheepfolds to the hill,
> if by chance you see
> him I love most,
> tell him I am sick, I suffer, and I die.

The only messengers available at this time are *our desires, affections, and longings for God*—yearnings that both nourish our commitment and show God the quality and early intensity of our dedication. However, we will still lack the knowledge, possession, and love of God we want. This is an important learning experience, as God teaches us that the intellect fails to know God, the memory fails to possess God, and the will fails to love God. We may have thought that all three faculties would help, but they all lead us astray from a true knowledge of God. Rather, we must learn that these three needs are connected to the theological virtues of faith, hope, and charity. God does not respond to these needs but creates them.

No doubt we want to do absolutely everything that is possible to *bring ourselves closer to God and to the values and vision of a life given to God*. This includes the practice of virtue and the fostering of deeper prayer, and along with these efforts goes the challenge to constantly focus on God and to withdrawal from all that is not God. We cannot allow self-satisfaction or self-centeredness to develop in this search, for this satisfaction itself can become an obstacle to further discovery of God. Rather we must give a total commitment to the exclusive focus on the search for God and for God's will. In this search we must withstand all the usual distractions and temptations that assail any person who seeks to focus his or her life of God. Among these problems are fear and anxiety at what others might think of us when we choose to focus more intensely on a God-directed life. Then there are the perennial temptations to slip back, or to be unfaithful to our commitment, or to lack the courage to persevere. So, the poet speaks of the threats and desires and hopes to avoid them.

> Seeking my Love
> I will head for the mountains and for watersides,
> I will not gather flowers,
> nor fear wild beasts;
> I will go beyond strong men and frontiers.

This first stage in our journey to deeper knowledge and love of God concludes with *our awareness of God's self-revelation in the wonders of the created world*. We discover how all aspects of creation reveal the wonders of God's love, and this awesome diversity leads us to deeper love of God.

> O woods and thickets,
> planted by the hand of my Beloved!
> O green meadow,
> coated, bright, with flowers,
> tell me, has he passed by you?
>
> Pouring out a thousand graces,
> he passed these groves in haste;
> and having looked at them,

with his image alone,
clothed them in beauty.

Longing for clearer knowledge of the Beloved (Stanzas 6-12)

The poem began with a cry for love, but now it continues with a cry for illumination and deeper knowledge to enrich love. The future bride says she has had enough of mere messages, stammerings, false concepts, emptiness, miseries, and half-hearted understandings. Rather, she wants to see her Beloved face to face. "She asks him that from henceforth he no longer detain her with any other knowledge, communications, and traces of his excellence since, rather than bringing her satisfaction, these increase her longings and suffering" (C. 6.2). So, the beginnings of the spiritual life are filled with trials of bitterness, mortification, and meditation, and the person who longs for knowledge of God can claim, "Among all worldly delights and sensible satisfactions and spiritual gratification and sweetness, there is certainly nothing with the power to heal me, nothing to satisfy me" (C. 6.3).

However, with stanza six there is a significant change, for here the future bride enters contemplation, and it is now God who draws her to an appreciation of the divine presence in creation (C. 6.1). In the earlier part (stanzas 1-5) the future bride tries to learn how to journey to God in love, now God becomes her teacher, transforming her in contemplation. The journey in the *Spiritual Canticle* is one in which God's love gradually purifies, illumines, and transforms the lover, helping her to control appetites, to learn how to love, and to be transformed in union. John moves so quickly to focus on contemplation that he gives the impression that the *Spiritual Canticle* is directed to those who are already in a contemplative prayer experience (C. Prologue.3). For John the goal of contemplative life is union with God in love; this is the transformation in God for which one longs. At this stage, it is illuminative, but also painful.

The world's beauty calls a person to love God, for God clothed the world in beauty to reflect the beauty of the Son, and this inspires each of us to love God. But this is painful too, for one still wants to possess God and be possessed by God in loving union and not just see signs of God's presence (C. 6.6). However, while the bride-to-be experiences urgent longings for her Beloved, he seems distant and passive; he stirs up love and then hides to intensify the bride's longings. When the bride tries to get close, the Beloved flees. Eventually the bride realizes that all is the work of the Beloved who draws her forward to greater love and illumines her regarding who he is and the nature of true love. While a person gains knowledge of God through irrational creatures, he or she also gains illumination through other rational creatures who reveal more about God than irrational ones do.

This further knowledge causes both love and pain. This is because while one appreciates God's self-communication through creatures as a love-filled experience, it is only partial while one is restricted to bodily life, and one yearns for greater union that can only come in the next life. The illumination is painful, like a wound, a deep sore, and even death—all part of impatient love (C. 7.2-4). So, overwhelmed by God's love, one seeks deeper union and realizes only God can heal this love-sickness. At this point one longs intensely for union with God and finds no satisfaction in anything else. He or she appreciates that love seems unfulfilled, and in fact, nothing can satisfy a person except God's gift of love (C. 8.2). A person now seeks God in all things and, as he or she abandons interest in everything else, God comes close in love. John's work is a mysticism of love. There is no cure for love-sickness except in the vision of God. Such a person feels God has called him or her to love, but is left feeling incomplete. "Such is the truly loving heart. The soul experiencing this love exclaims: 'Why do you leave it so,' that is, empty, hungry, alone, sorely wounded and sick with love, suspended in the air, and fail to carry off what you have stolen?" (C. 9.6).

The bride in the poem feels in need of healing, for nothing satisfies her, and everything becomes burdensome except the pursuit of love. "A characteristic of the desires of love is that all deeds and words unconformed with what the will loves will weary, tire, annoy, and displease the soul as she beholds that her desire goes unfulfilled" (C. 10.5). A person longs for this intimate revelation of God's inner life of beauty, and once God gives a glimpse of divine beauty he or she would do anything to see that vision again (C. 11.2). Such a person knows the teachings of faith but longs for the substance of faith in a clear vision of God (C. 12.4-5), when the truths are infused by God's transforming presence. One feels the intensity of longing; feels so close and yet not quite there. "The more the object of her desire comes into sight and the closer it draws, while still being denied her, so much more pain and torment does it cause" (C. 12.9). Illumination is no longer enough, the bride longs for union.

Reflections on the text

The second phase in the spiritual journey focuses on illumination—gaining more knowledge of God and of our own call to love. Having appreciated signs and assurances of our own commitment in our desires, hopes, and longings, we realize these are not enough to heal our pain and to satisfy our longings for knowledge and love of God. They seem like messengers when we want an encounter with the one we seek.

> Ah, who has the power to heal me?
> now wholly surrender yourself!
> Do not send me
> any more messengers,
> they cannot tell me what I must hear.

The beauty and richness of creation reveal so many traces of God's love, but we will not be satisfied with these signs of God's extraordinary generosity. Authentic love can only be satisfied in mutual presence and union. Everything else seems partial and inadequate and increases sorrow at God's absence rather than bring joy. It is useful at this early stage to appreciate that nothing in this world, no matter how wonderful, can satisfy the deep longings we feel for transforming love. Certainly, creation gives glimpses of God's love, and so too will many exceptional men and women we meet who can share with us their thrill in knowing and loving God. We may even be moved at the thought of God's generous love in the Incarnation and experience intense moments of God's enduring love in our lives. But we will always want a more direct encounter, and all else will be unsatisfying.

> All who are free,
> tell me a thousand graceful things of you;
> all wound me more
> and leave me dying
> of, ah, I-don't-know-what behind their stammering.

The more we get to know God, the more we will want to be in intense union with God, but we *will feel bound and restricted by the limitations of our mortal life.* Our longings will overwhelm us, as God's knowledge and love penetrate our inner spirit, and we will even feel we cannot endure the separation.

> How do you endure
> O life, not living where you live,
> and being brought near death
> by the arrows you receive
> from that which you conceive of your Beloved?

Only God can fully satisfy our longings and heal our pain. Brief encounters with the Lover leave us with more pain than joy, broken-hearted rather than satisfied. But we will find we are constantly thinking of God and God's love for us, and these longings will increase. Love longs for more love until the longing for fulfillment brings complete, satisfying love.

> Why since you wounded
> this heart, don't you heal it?
> And why, since you stole it from me,

> do you leave it so,
> and fail to carry off what you have stolen?

At this time *we will long for healing of this lovesickness.* Nothing else will satisfy us, not even incomplete, partial love. We will find we want to abandon all other desires and small loves to focus exclusively on seeking knowledge and love of God. This centering of all on God prepares us for the union we seek.

> Extinguish these miseries,
> since no one else can stamp them out
> and may my eyes behold you,
> because you are their light,
> and I would open them to you alone.

As our love intensifies and our pursuit becomes relentless, *God will often grant us glimpses of the beauty of the divine presence.* Our experience of God's loving union and presence of beauty will bring us the healing we seek.

> Reveal your presence,
> and may the vision of your beauty be my death;
> for the sickness of love
> is not cured
> except by your presence and image.

The period of illumination brings transformation and a profound realization that we must seek union in the truth of faith. If the truth and substance of faith is like gold, then the propositions of faith are like silver, communicating God to us truly, even though covered with the restrictions of this life—an imperfect sketch in our hearts. Realizing this, we are ready for the next stage.

> O spring like crystal!
> If only, on your silvered-over faces,
> you would suddenly form

the eyes I have desired,
which I bear sketched deep within my heart.

The unitive stage – part I; spiritual betrothal (Stanzas 13-21)

Once the lover arrives at this stage in his or her spiritual journey, the will is purified and now focused on love for God alone, as the lover gives her total "yes" to God in love and in the desire for union (see F. 3.24). This total giving of self to God is a critical junction in the spiritual life and readies one for God's special gifts of grace (C. 13.1). This looks like a journey the future bride is making to find her Beloved, but it is a journey that the lover and God make together for human efforts need the support of grace. The period of spiritual engagement is an in-breaking of God's transforming love and includes special knowledge of God and of God's loving presence, as well as gifts and virtues for the lover. "[T]his spiritual flight denotes a high state and union of love in which, after much spiritual exercise, the soul is placed by God. This state is called spiritual betrothal with the Word, the Son of God" (C. 14-15.2). This period of betrothal prepares the soul for spiritual marriage where total transformation takes place. The future bride feels protected from previous disturbances, but also feels the pain of the absence of the Beloved, of the pain he causes in her heart and of his touches of love that pierce and burn like arrows. Even the special love-filled communications cause pain, for the body cannot sustain the intensity of this experience (C. 13.2, 4).

At this point in the journey, the bride-to-be longs to be outside of the restrictions of this present life, but the Lover, who speaks for the first time in stanza 13, urges her to remain in the struggles and growth of this life where she can give time to further purification, to increased preparation, and to learning how to love in a new way. At this time God communicates in contemplation new knowledge that leads to deeper love (C. 13.10-11). The future bride, called to return to her Lover, sings of the Lover's greatness and praises, senses an end to unfulfilled love, is refreshed with special communications of God's grandeur, delight, gentleness, and peaceful love, and sees the loving presence of God in the harmony of creation (C. 14-15.2). The desire for union with God is intensified, and God passively communicates spiritual revelations.

Spiritual betrothal is a high level of union in love, when God communicates knowledge and extraordinary gifts. It is also a time of peace, quiet, and enjoyment without the former pain. It is passive illumination concerning God's wisdom and love in creation, a period of vital experiences of the attributes of God, and an awareness that God is personally transforming a person. At this time he or she is possessed by the transforming power of God—an awesome experience, but without the fear and trembling of former times (C. 14-15.30). This is a knowledge that nourishes, refreshes, and deepens love—gifts of divine communication that are received passively in contemplation. It is an experience of mutuality that makes the *Spiritual Canticle* different from the *Ascent* and the *Dark Night*. Moreover, all this is now at the level of the spiritual faculties only—the intellect, memory, and will. Still, all kinds of evil tendencies can disrupt the loving and delightful union. Even though a person may have sensory appetites under control, disturbances can still come, and he or she soon realizes nothing can be done without God's help (C. 16.2-3).

The seeker feels pain when the Beloved is absent and when disturbances affect the focus on love. "The reason for such affliction is that since she has a singular and intense love for God in this state, his absence is a singular and intense torment for her" (C. 17.1). The Holy Spirit draws such a person out of aridity—the unfelt experience of God and the lack of consolation in prayer—while encouraging one to remember the beauty of a life of virtue (C. 17.2). A person now sees and appreciates his or her own gifts, yet knows union remains incomplete (C. 18.1). Suffering remains from the threat of sensory rebellions that can disturb one's peace, and the person should pray that God protect him or her at this time (C. 18.3-4).

A person now asks that all divine communication be only with the spiritual faculties. This request that one's intellect, memory, and will be transformed is pleasing to God who responds by communicating special knowledge to these spiritual parts. Now, the intellect can be directed by faith, the memory by hope, and the will by charity. "Since the soul desires the highest and most excellent communications from God, and is unable to receive them in the company of the sensory part, she desires God to bestow them apart from it" (C. 19.1). Now, a person longs for the next stage in the spiritual life, spiritual marriage. This development requires further purification which the Beloved promises to achieve in his future bride (C. 20-21.1). He gives peace and tranquility, controls the faculties, and brings to an end the negative effects of the passions (C. 20-21.16).

Reflections on the text

The closer you come to God but are not totally transformed in love, the more *you will feel pain, emptiness, and darkness until totally transformed in love*. The problem is that weak humanity cannot endure the in-breaking of God's purifying and transforming love. While the seeker wants total union he or she will feel one of two reactions; either to ask God to withdraw because one cannot deal with the intensity of the love, or to ask God to draw one to the life of the spirit where a person can cope with this intense love. In the poem the Bridegroom chooses the former for the bride and grants special gifts of gentleness, peace, and love so the bride will not be disturbed by this union in love.

> Withdraw them, Beloved,
> I am taking flight!
> Return, dove,
> the wounded stag
> is in sight on the hill,
> cooled by the breeze of your flight.

If you are one who is blessed by God to reach this stage you will enter new levels of blessings. *In this union you will see everything through the lens of love* and because of your love you will see the whole world differently. This new commitment in spiritual betrothal or engagement removes some of the pain of unfulfilled longings and replaces them with peaceful communication. This is a glimpse of divine life and a profound awareness of the personal transforming presence of God in your life. Every aspect of life now speaks to you of God's love. This new illumination makes you aware of the wonderful harmony God has placed in every part of creation.

> My Beloved, the mountains,
> and lonely wooded valleys,
> strange islands,
> and resounding rivers,
> the whistling of love-stirring breezes,
>
> the tranquil night
> at the time of the rising dawn,
> silent music,
> sounding solitude,
> the supper that refreshes, and deepens love.

It is natural at this time that you will not want any disturbances to disrupt the union you feel. When these temptations arise like snappy foxes to thwart and contradict the loving union, refocus on God's gifts and re-commit yourself to God in solitude and peace.

> Catch us the foxes,
> for our vineyard is now in flower,
> while we fashion a cone of roses
> intricate as the pine's;
> and let no one appear on the hill.

Once you have tasted the joy of loving union you will feel intensely its absences. Any disturbance, no matter how small or brief, gives rise to fear of losing the gifts you enjoy. Spiritual dryness is like a deadening north wind, when you prefer the awakening love of the Holy Spirit who acts like a warm south wind that brings further love, refreshes your spirit, increases your life of virtue, and prepares you for further transformation. At this time both you and your great Lover are mutually nourished by this love.

> Be still, deadening north wind;
> south wind come, you that waken love,
> breathe through my garden,
> let its fragrance flow,
> and the Beloved will feed amid the flowers.

Since your union in love is not yet total *you will still deal with temptations*, bad appetites, inordinate sensory rebellions that will threaten and disquiet peaceful union. You may feel surrounded and imprisoned by these disturbances and hope they will just stay away and not come near you.

> You girls of Judea,
> while among flowers and roses
> the amber spreads its perfume,
> stay away, there on the outskirts:
> do not so much as seek to touch our thresholds.

Now is the time to desire no further communication through the senses that can always be threatened by distractions, but only communication to the spiritual, hidden part of your inner spirit. There *in secret God imparts special knowledge to the intellect in faith, divine love to the will, and takes possession of the memory in hope.*

> Hide yourself, my love;
> turn your face toward the mountains,
> and do not speak;
> but look at those companions
> going with her through strange islands.

At this point in the journey of love, as you approach and make final preparations for spiritual marriage, *you can concentrate on expressing your true "yes" of love to God.* God grants peace, conforms all aspects of your life to the life of the Spirit. God also controls for you the wanderings of the imagination, anger, and concupiscence. God perfects the direction of the spiritual faculties of intellect, memory, and will. God brings an end to the negative effects of the four passions of sorrow, hope, joy, and fear. You can now rest in God's peace and enjoy the sleep of love.

> Swift-winged birds,
> lions, stags, and leaping roes,
> mountains, lowlands, and river banks,
> waters, winds, and ardors,
> watching fears of night:
>
> By the pleasant lyres,
> and the siren's song, I conjure you
> to cease your anger
> and not touch the wall,
> that the bride may sleep in deeper peace.

The unitive way—part II; spiritual marriage (Stanzas 22-40)

A. A DESCRIPTION OF TOTAL UNION IN SPIRITUAL MARRIAGE (Stanzas 22-35).

This part begins with the bride peacefully resting in the arms of her Beloved, while the Bridegroom tells the bride that his transformation of her began under the tree of the cross in redemptive grace. This transformation continues now through his work of helping her control all negative effects of the lower appetites and thus helping her enter a new level of existence. So, spiritual marriage is a profound transformation of the person. "This spiritual marriage is incomparably greater than the spiritual betrothal, for it is a total transformation in the Beloved, in which each surrenders the entire possession of self to the other with a certain consummation of the union of love" (C. 22.3). It is an experience of peaceful security, mutual surrender, and equality in love. It focuses on love alone in mutual self-gift. God makes all this possible, for God is love, and here the Bridegroom's love is the point of departure (C. 22.1). God purifies former failures, and this leads to mutual gratitude and rejoicing for both lovers.

In spiritual marriage the beloved and the Lover surrender themselves to each other, and they become one. The Lover reveals special secrets and a deeper appreciation of the divine mysteries of the Incarnation and Redemption. He also shows how he personally redeemed each one and raised each one up to renewed life. Thus, in spiritual marriage the whole of human nature is harmoniously integrated (C. 22). This is a time to peacefully enjoy the gifts of union with one's Lover, and celebrate the awareness of the many gifts and virtues that God places in the soul. There develops an equality of friendship, a mature relationship with God, and the beloved now participates in divine life (C. 28.1).

This is also a time when the bride in the story also praises and celebrates the many gifts God has bestowed on others (C. 25.1-5). A person sees, welcomes, and celebrates how God encourages others, inflames them with love, fills them with charity, and matures their love. At the same time, the beloved rests secure in the transforming presence of God for, with God's grace, she has now controlled all negative disturbances of appetites, and she experiences immersion in the most intimate love possible in this life. "[T]he soul relates the sovereign favor God granted by recollecting her in the intimacy of his love, which is the union with God, or transformation, through love. And she notes two effects of this union: forgetfulness or withdrawal from all worldly things, and mortification of all her appetites and gratifications" (C. 26.2).

In this contemplative union God and the beloved mutually surrender themselves to each other, and God communicates a mystical knowledge to his bride that transforms all her spiritual faculties, drawing them exclusively to divine life. "The sweet and living knowledge that she says he taught her is mystical theology, the secret knowledge of God that spiritual people call contemplation. This knowledge is very delightful because it is a knowledge through love" (C. 27.5). Thus, God raises the seeker to the level of equality in love, and in response a person dedicates all his or her energies to love; everything is now done for love (C. 28.7). Such a person appreciates that attentiveness to God and to the practice of love is the only focus of life, and leaves aside interest in everything else as ends in themselves to focus exclusively on the love of God and to integrate every aspect of life into this love. In this communion each one finds his or her true purpose and destiny in life. In this mutual sharing, communion, and love, the beloved and God enjoy each other's self-gift (C. 30.2). Such a one can see how all his or her virtues, struggles, and efforts are the result of God's gifts, but somehow God values them as the beloved's efforts to become worthy of God and as a proof of love.

Then, too, a person's life of virtue is an image of God whose love has made all this possible. Now, such a person and God are bound together in strong love (C. 31.3). However, God's love is also purifying, cleansing one from all former failures. A faith-filled seeker is aware of this transformation that God has wrought and so takes no credit for the growth but attributes all to God. This humble acknowledgement makes one more appealing to God. This relationship of friendship and love leads both God and the person to mutual gratitude (C. 34.1). God celebrates the beloved's growth and commitment, and the beloved rests in contemplative union, refreshed, protected, and blessed by God. God celebrates the beloved's peace, love, and happiness, and God praises the seeker's withdrawal into solitude away from every other satisfaction. The beloved has found what he or she sought and is now alone in God. This spiritual marriage is a direct communication of divine love.

Reflections on the text

Your spiritual journey up to this point has consisted in *God striving to free you from all the evil tendencies* you may have, to dispel dryness in your spiritual life, and to increase your love for God and neighbor. At this point you enter the union of spiritual marriage—the total transformation in the love of God. This mutual surrender is a new level of existence for you and you can delight in this union.

> The bride has entered
> the sweet garden of her desire,
> and she rests in delight,
> laying her neck
> on the gentle arms of her Beloved.

In this union the Beloved communicates wonderful divine secrets, including deeper appreciation of the mysteries of the Incarnation and Redemption. This gift of insight must be complemented by a progressive response on your part of striving for union.

> Beneath the apple tree:
> there I took you for my own,
> there I offered you my hand,
> and restored you,
> where your mother was corrupted.

One who reaches this stage enjoys the graces and blessings of the Beloved in peace and security, celebrating the perfect love he or she has been seeking. One now feels protected from former evils and filled with peace and tranquility. This is a special time to enjoy God's presence and to receive special communications of divine knowledge.

> Our bed is in flower,
> bound round with linking dens of lions,
> hung with purple,
> built up in peace,
> and crowned with a thousand shields of gold.

Among the special gifts of the Beloved *you will find support to pursue a life conformed to God's will*, an enflaming of love in your heart, and an abundance of charity. These will lead you to respond with increased desire, love, and praise of God—signs of mature love.

> Following your footprints
> maidens run along the way;
> the touch of a spark,
> the spiced wine,
> cause flowings in them from the balsam of God.

You can now rest secure in God's presence and feel the transforming love of God deep within your inner spirit. In this transformation God communicates divine revelations to the very center of your being, grants divine wisdom, and transforms your love into divine love. This immersion in God leads you to be absorbed in the love for God and disinterested in all else—although some useless distractions will still remain and bother you.

> In the inner wine cellar
> I drank of my Beloved, and, when I went abroad
> through all this valley
> I no longer knew anything,
> and lost the herd which I was following.

God now communicates with you in extraordinary intimacy, tenderness, and even humility, leading you to want to respond in complete surrender of yourself to God. *In this mutual surrender God teaches secret divine wisdom*—a love-filled mystical knowledge.

This will lead you to center all your actions, cares, and fidelity on God's will alone and nothing else.

> There he gave me his breast;
> there he taught me a sweet and living knowledge;
> and I gave myself to him,
> keeping nothing back;
> there I promised to be his bride.

Every aspect of your life is now centered on love of God. Intellect, memory, and will, along with the energies of the sensory part, are focused on the service of God—even when you may be unaware of it. All you do is now done for love.

> Now I occupy my soul
> and all my energy in his service;
> I no longer tend the herd,
> nor have I any other work
> now that my every act is love.

At this time *your priority will be the exclusive focus on intimate love of God* in prayer, and you will find that even dedication to the service of others will be very secondary. People may conclude you seem a little lost, but you have actually found your true self—absorbed in the love of God.

> If, then, I am no longer
> seen or found on the common,
> you will say that I am lost;
> That, stricken by love,
> I lost myself, and was found.

Clearly, *this is a time of mutual love and appreciation.* The Beloved endows the bride in the story with many gifts and virtues— gifts for sure, but also results of the lover's constant and courageous efforts throughout the journey. Virtues given and acquired are all bound together by love, and without love they have no value. These virtues make the lover more attractive in God's sight.

> With flowers and emeralds
> chosen on cool mornings
> we shall weave garlands
> flowering in your love,
> and bound with one hair of mine.

Endowed with many virtues, the bride appears more and more like the Beloved. So *united in love, the two lovers seem one.* God rejoices in the bride's strong love. After years of efforts and purification, the bride's love for God is now detached, strong, unbreakable, and captivating in its faith and fidelity. This love is the result of the transformation of the spiritual faculties and the resulting union is now in the intellect, memory, and will enriched by faith, hope, and charity.

> You considered
> that one hair fluttering at my neck;
> you gazed at it upon my neck
> and it captivated you;
> and one of my eyes wounded you.

The power and tenacity of the bride's love binds her to God and *both mutually surrender to each other.* This love is all gift; God gave this love and faith and thus made the bride worthy and capable of divine love. Elevated by God's grace the bride appreciates that everything is God's gift. She sees God in a new way and celebrates the wonder of God's love.

> When you looked at me
> your eyes imprinted your grace in me;
> for this you loved me ardently;
> and thus my eyes deserved
> to adore what they beheld in you.

Part of God's transforming love is to remove all former sin from the bride's past life. While she rejoices in the mercy and renewed dignity, she *should not forget former failures* for this transformation is unmerited. Yet God is now captivated by the bride's new beauty, celebrates it, and endows her with more gifts.

> Do not despise me;
> for if, before, you found me dark,
> now truly you can look at me
> since you have looked
> and left in me grace and beauty.

The relationship of friendship and of indescribable love leads the bride to gratitude, praise, and refreshment in this love. She has discovered what she always longed for and rejoices in this fulfillment and peace.

> The small white dove
> has returned to the ark with an olive branch;
> and now the turtledove
> has found its longed-for mate

Settled in God and God in her, the bride has no further needs. She enters union with God in her solitude away from every other satisfaction. *Now she finds true love in God alone.* In this experience of spiritual marriage God communicates directly with his bride without intermediaries. Their mutual gift of love is now complete. God is now in union with his bride, guides her, and absorbs her in himself.

B. THE SOUL STILL LONGS FOR PERFECT UNION WITH THE BELOVED IN GLORY (Stanzas 36-40).

These last stanzas describe the state of the blessed in their lives beyond the present one to which the perfect now aspire. John goes on to describe the two lovers' longing for total union in the life beyond this one (C. 36.3). This includes immersion and participation in the mysteries of God, delight, gratitude, and complete harmony in union with God. Like two lovers, God and the beloved enjoy each other's company and long for ever deeper union. The bride rejoices in the communications of love, wants them to permeate every aspect of life, and longs to become a reflection of the beauty of God, even if this means suffering or death. In fact, such a person longs for this life to end in order to enjoy the mysteries of God. Even now, he or she vitally experiences the attributes of God and the wonderful ways of God, and is transformed and inebriated by God's love (C. 37.5). Each one can delight in these experiences and gratefully give glory to God. Lovers always want to love as much as they are loved, and the beloved again asks God to reveal and to teach how to love. The beloved surrenders to God in love, and God transforms and perfects this love. He or she desires "to reach the consummation of the love of God, which she had always been seeking; that is, to love God as purely and perfectly as he loves her in order to repay him by such love" (C. 38.2).

The lover is overwhelmed by this transforming vision which is a contemplative vision of the divine essence and an immersion in the love of God, when one becomes God through participation. "Yet God accomplishes this in the soul through communication and participation. This is transformation in the three Persons in power and wisdom and love, and thus the soul is like God through this transformation" (C. 39.4). This is a foretaste of what is to come in the next life. This is human destiny—to be free of all that is not God, to be taught a new knowledge of God, and to be transformed by perfect and strong love. A person's entire being is now in harmony with the Spirit. Looking back over life, a person can see former failures, appreciate the divine transformation, welcome the joy felt in one's entire being, and ask that God continue these blessings of spiritual marriage to the glorious celebration of marriage in the next life. Yet, there is no closure to the *Spiritual Canticle* for there is no end to desire in this life.

Reflections on the text

The two lovers want to be together in their intimate love and want nothing and no one to disturb their love. They appreciate that *the limitations of this life prevent total union*, and so they long for that final step. Even now they want to savor the joy of their love, become more and more like each other, and learn more about each other even their deepest secrets.

> Let us rejoice, Beloved,
> and let us go forth to behold ourselves in your beauty
> to the mountain and to the hill
> to where the pure water flows,
> and further, deep into the thicket.

They long to be with each other in deep union. *The lover vitally experiences the attributes of God* and experiences the revelation of hidden mysteries of God. The Beloved and the lover enter these new revelations together for the bride no longer does anything on her own. This transformation leads to further delight and praise, as God continues to reveal to the bride mysteries, divine judgment, and overflowing knowledge of God's attributes, wonders, and greatness.

> And then we will go on
> to the high caverns in the rock
> which are so well concealed;
> there we shall enter
> and taste the fresh juice of the pomegranates.

The bride delights in being immersed in the wisdom of God. She wants to express her love even more and realizes this is not possible until she passes beyond the restrictions of this life. Even now, she understands, possesses, and loves in and through God, uniting her intellect, memory, and will with God. She wants to love God as perfectly as God loves her.

> There you will show me
> what my soul has been seeking,
> and then you will give me,
> you, my life, will give me there
> what you gave me on that other day.

The bride enjoys the total transformation God brings her. *Now she understands, knows, and loves through the power of the Trinity* within her, and she has by participation what the Lover has by nature. In her rejoicing the bride understands total union is for the next life.

> The breathing of the air,
> the song of the sweet nightingale,
> the grove and its living beauty
> in the serene night
> with a flame that is consuming and painless.

The bride now lives in total harmony with God and asks that God continue to confirm these blessings. All evil of former times no longer has power over her. The joy she now finds in this union of love overflows to every aspect of her life and draws sense to appreciate the joy of inner recollection.

> No one looked at her,
> nor did Aminadab appear;
> the siege was still;
> and the cavalry,
> at the sight of the waters, descended.

This journey of love in the *Spiritual Canticle* offers a revolutionary vision of our approach to the stages of the spiritual journey. This is not a journey of a lonely, struggling person in search of the unseen God. This is not a solitary pursuit of wisdom, a desire to be alone before the alone. Moreover, it does not focus on self-denial and asceticism as an exclusively negative way to God. "Where have you hidden, Beloved?" indicates from the first line that this is a journey that two lovers make together. Love is present from the beginning, as we travel in union with the Beloved. This is a rich, fulfilling, exciting journey that we undertake with warmth, excitement, and enthusiasm. Love, of course, always needs to be strong, and lovers are always ready to sacrifice in order to prove their love and deepen it. John, the doctor of divine and human love, turns so much former spirituality upside down, reminding us that in this journey God, in love, is accompanying us all the way, in fact, is simply taking us home.

Chapter 5
Accepting the pain of love with courage
Reflections on the Dark Night

Beginners' immature love (Passive night of the senses)

    Mistaking self-love for real love

    Changing the focus of love

Making a serious commitment in love (passive night of spirit)

    Letting God love in us and teach us how to love

    Welcoming the pain of love

    Appreciating the benefits of true love

    Understanding the characteristics of authentic spiritual love

It is common to consider that John presents his readers with the journey of faith in the *Ascent* and the *Dark Night*, and the journey of love in the *Spiritual Canticle* and the *Living Flame of*

Love. However, he tells us that the purpose of the *Dark Night* is to describe a person's conduct "along the spiritual road that leads to the perfect union with God through love" (N. Title). Of course, one only undertakes this journey when one is "fired with love's urgent longings," and one travels "with no other light or guide than the one that burned in my heart," and at the end of the journey, it is "love alone," that makes one soar to God (N.2. 25.4). Perhaps we could describe the *Dark Night* as the journey of strong love (N.2. 11.3; see C. 31.4). From start to end John's approach is "nor have I any other work now that my every act is love" (C. v. 28), and overriding every other conviction is "When evening comes you will be examined in love" (S. 60).

Introduction

John's own experience of the dark night during the time spent in the Toledo prison unquestionably forms the background to his book on the *Dark Night*. Abandoned, in poverty, emptiness, rejection, and pain, he reaffirms his faith in the absolute otherness of God. It is remarkable in its own way to recall that John's dark night in Toledo produced his greatest love poem, the *Spiritual Canticle*, also the most extraordinary synthesis of God's love for humanity described in the *Romances*, and also the haunting reaffirmation of faith and love in the poem "For I know well the spring that flows and runs." John's experience of darkness produced the love, beauty, and gratitude that characterize profound faith. Darkness led to illumination, and the pain of purifying contemplation transformed his entire life, centering it on love.

Some writers have thought that John wrote the poem, "One Dark Night," while in prison, but that is most unlikely. Rather, he probably wrote the poem in El Calvario or Beas, certainly in light of the prison experience (see A.1. 15.1 and N.2. 14.1) and most likely within a year of that experience. Perhaps, more than any other mystic, John gave beautiful poetic expression to his experience. There is an extraordinary power in the poem, "One Dark Night." It is real; does not come from someone's imagination, but rather is an expression of John's personal experience. However, it is an experience that many men and women undergo, clearly to a lesser degree, and they find John's articulation touches them, genuinely and authentically. We have all encountered darkness and emptiness, and when we read John's mystical language it becomes suggestive of our own struggles and searches. Of course, one can read "One Dark Night" at different times in life, and each time it means something different as our own experiences deepen, the darkness becomes more painful, and the illumination more transforming.

John refers to the poem as "Songs of the soul that rejoices in having reached . . . union with God, by the path of spiritual negation." When John refers to "negation" he is making a very positive statement. He means a person has reached a state of union by emphasizing exclusively the search for union and love and has been willing to deny anything that could hinder the exclusive focus on the love of God. So, the poem is written after one has come through this journey of the dark night and been taught new levels of love. There are eight stanzas which highlight the various stages in the journey from the dark night, glad night, guiding night, night more lovely than the dawn, to a night that has united the Lover with his beloved. There are three tempos or rhythms to the poem. The first three stanzas—which are the ones John comments on in detail—are quiet and calming, "my house being now all stilled." With the fourth stanza we are introduced to a new exciting tempo, continued in the fifth; an excitement of search, encounter, and transformation. The last three stanzas speak of peaceful satisfaction, shared love, and loving abandonment. All this takes place in darkness. Book One of the *Dark Night* comments on the first stanza, focusing on the nature of the passive night of sense. Book Two utilizes stanza one to describe the passive night of spirit, stanza two to highlight the various characteristics of contemplation during the passive night of spirit, and stanza three to outline the properties of the passive night of spirit. In the *Dark Night* John describes the rigorous transformation by God of a person who is open, ready, and willing to receive and to respond to this call. It is an uncompromising battle against selfishness and self-centered love to prepare one for transformed love in union with God.

In writing the *Dark Night*, John gives helpful advice, suggests stages of growth that can be helpful in one's theological understanding and in spiritual direction, but insists they are fluid and very individual. "Not everyone undergoes this in the same way" (N.1. 14.5). "It is better to explain the utterances of love in their broadest sense so that each one may derive profit from them according to the mode and capacity of one's own spirit" (C. Prologue.2). Moreover, the journey of the *Dark Night* is not spiritual purification or endurance alone, but a love-motivated journey to union. John constantly calls us to search for total commitment to union with God in love, and to be willing to make the sacrifices necessary to gain the All. This is not primarily a journey of denial but of love and courageous affirmation of one's true self—the discovery of who God is calling one to be.

In his presentation of the dynamic development of the spiritual life John was originally considered a disciple of Pseudo-Dyonisius the Areopagite, who divided the spiritual life into three main stages: beginners, proficients, and perfect, corresponding to the purgative, illuminative, and unitive periods of spiritual life. Writers dependent on this insight generally considered the three stages to be important but rarely gave any importance to the transitions from one stage to another. John's own experience, together with extensive knowledge gained through spiritual direction, gave him better insight into the stages than anyone prior to him. To the traditional three-fold division John highlights the two crucial transitions. John knew from his own experience of night that crises can be moments of grace and progress, and he called the two transitions the night of the senses and the night of spirit. The former was the transition to contemplation, and the latter the decisive moment of life as the complete trusting abandonment to God. The three stages of prior understandings remain and the second becomes a plateau of rest between the nights.

Thus, the nights become so important that John describes the entire journey to God as a dark night. Dedicated people who have started the journey come to a point where they advance no more. The problem is clear to John; for one reason or another they do not abandon themselves to God's guidance and enter the dark night. "[A] soul must ordinarily pass through two principal kinds of nights. . . . The first night or purgation . . . concerns the sensory part of the soul. The second night. . . concerns the spiritual part" (A.1. 1.1-2). Both nights have an active part and a passive part. John presents the active nights in the *Ascent* and the passive nights in the *Dark Night*.

Reflections on the text

In our spiritual journey there comes a time when *we enter the thick darkness where we encounter God* (Ex 20:21), and God gradually turns our darkness into light (Is 42:16). The journey through the passive nights is entirely in the hands of God. "In the first place it should be known that if anyone is seeking God, the Beloved is seeking that person much more" (F. 3.28). The point of departure is not our efforts but a loving God who is drawing us through the darkness to the light (N.1. 1.1; N.2. 1.1).

This is a journey that consists in the pursuit of nothing--no thing, a new discipline that we impose on ourselves or allow and undergo in God. John speaks of the nothingness of all creation in comparison with God and of all created and spiritual things as means to union with God. It is not that he despises any of them but that he sees everything as nothing in relation to God (N.1. 4.4-7). This can be a disconcerting aspect of John's teaching unless we constantly remember his goal of everything re-found in God; through poverty and nakedness in God we possess all (see "Prayer of a soul taken with love").

Poverty and negation, or mortification of voluntary, habitual imperfections that move us away from God are *means to liberate us from what is false in ourselves, in our world, and in our understanding of God* (A.1. 11). We have a role to pay in this purification as John describes in the *Ascent*, but the great work of liberation is done for us by God's transforming interventions described in the *Dark Night*. This becomes a spiritual empowerment and gives us the freedom to choose the good, to eliminate all that is not of God, and to pursue eagerly only what is of God. Thus, we become dry and ready to be set on fire. "For to love is to labor to divest and deprive oneself for God of all that is not God" (A.2. 5.7). All these efforts are then complemented and enriched by God's work within us in the passive nights.

Beginners' immature love (Passive night of the senses)

Mistaking self-love for real love

The passive night of sense describes beginners' imperfections and their need of the dark night to purify them. It points to the methods they use and how and when with God's help they can transition to the next stage. A common problem in the spiritual life arises when people focus on religion for the satisfaction it gives them rather than on the challenge and conversion to which it calls. At this time, the love they think they evidence is self-love—an enjoyment and satisfaction they feel. Such people mean well but they need God's help to redirect their lives and commitment with the experience of the dark night.

The passive night of the senses consists in a process of purification and re-education of the senses caused by the illumination of contemplation by which the senses are accommodated to the spirit. This is a passive night that affects beginners who have already dedicated themselves to God for some time and have been involved in the active night of purification of the senses (see A.1. 13.1). Having found satisfaction in the things of God, they have already tried to become detached from things that led away from God and are ready for God's further challenges. "God desires to withdraw them from this base manner of loving and lead them on to a higher degree of divine love. And he desires to liberate them from the lowly exercise of the senses and of discursive meditation" (N.1. 8.3). God does this by withdrawing all satisfaction these beginners find in their religious devotions. "This change is a surprise to them because everything seems to be functioning in reverse" (N.1. 8.3). Instead of the enjoyment and satisfaction they found in their religious devotions, they now find these same religious practices distasteful, and they feel empty and dissatisfied. Some may respond by working harder than ever at their discursive meditation, but this is not desirable. "They are like someone who turns from what has already been done in order to do it again" (N.1. 10.1). Others show a lot of conscious and unconscious resistance to God's love and illumination, and this needs the purification of actual, habitual, and socially justified sin. We often want ourselves more than we want God, and by clinging to our views of religious devotions we block God out of our lives.

John offers three signs that, when simultaneously present, indicate that a person is entering the passive night of sense. First, they cease to find any consolation, either from creatures or from the things of God. Second, they are pained by their own lack of service to God (see N.1. 9; also A.2. 13.2-4; A.2. 14). Third, these persons can no longer meditate as before, and have no desire to apply their imagination to formal discursive meditation, but rather find satisfaction in a quiet, loving attention toward God (A.2. 13.2-4). When these signs are present together, these people should leave meditation without fear and follow the Spirit, for God is leading them from meditation to contemplation (N.1. 10.1).

So, the passive night of the senses marks the transition from effort-filled meditation to peaceful, passive contemplation, the latter being God's transforming gift, which is light for the understanding and love for the will. "For contemplation is nothing else than a secret and peaceful and loving inflow of God, which, if not hampered, fires the soul in the spirit of love" (N.1. 10.6). This passive deprivation of the satisfactions of sense is accompanied by a new activity of the spirit, a new prayer, and a new faith (see A.2. 12.6-7). Since contemplation is incompatible with the images of meditation, one who contemplates cannot meditate and generally does not return to discursive prayer. Moreover, this contemplation can be illuminative and delightful, but also purgative and painful.

Reflections on the text

The dark night of the senses is only the entrance into that of spirit (see N.1. 14.1). Moreover, referring to the active night of spirit, John says, . . . "divine union is not perfected by this night alone" (A.3. 2.14), but only by the passive night of God's purifying interventions. Nowadays, the two aspects of the night—passive night of sense and active night of spirit—are generally experienced together, or at least they overlap. As the illumination of contemplation emphasizes the roots of faults, the active night must work to remove them.

We must still remind ourselves today that *nothing can adequately represent God*. Even religion's best efforts still fall short—they are idols in comparison to the reality and wonders of God, for God who is inscrutable does not conform to our images. "However impressive may be one's knowledge or experience of God, that knowledge or experience will have no resemblance to God and amount to very little" (A.2. 4.3). We must focus our love on who God is and not on some idol we have created.

John addresses *the method used during this journey, namely overcoming attachment to all things that we mistakenly think lead us to God* and abandoning any self-satisfaction we find in devotions. The beginning of the journey is a dark night caused by the purifying results of contemplation which passively reveal deeper levels of selfishness. If we have made this journey we can look back with satisfaction at our good fortune. Our love of God motivates us to make this journey while God's love, given in contemplation, passively begins to control inordinate passions of sense that can impede our way to true love.

Changing the focus of love

The book of the *Dark Night* describes the transition from beginners to proficients and the new approach to love that this implies. Beginners are in a lowly state (e.g. their prayer is meditation and their love is immature), but they should take courage and intensify their desire that God place them in the dark night which will strengthen them in virtue and prepare them for union with God in love. Beginners are already people who have resolutely committed themselves to God's service. God takes care of them and allows them to find increased satisfaction in their spiritual experiences. Beginners increase their spiritual devotions and find lots of satisfaction in them. But this is one of the weaknesses of beginners whose motivation becomes the consolation and satisfaction they experience, while many faults and imperfections remain unchecked, which can only be purified by the dark night.

In approaching the purification of the passive night of sense, John highlights the typical failures that need purifying, they are now somewhat hidden under the cover of spiritual dedication. So, remarkably, he deals with the seven deadly sins, all applied to spiritual weaknesses—focusing on sense satisfaction in religious devotions which leads to misguided love. Beginners cling to their religious devotions and pietistic supports just as others cling to the sensual versions of the seven deadly sins. Once again, John does not care whether you are attached to power or liturgy, sex or prayer forms, the only thing that matters is the heart's focus on self-satisfaction rather than on total dedication to God. All this must be purified through God's interventions in the passive night of sense.

Reflections on the text

When John discusses the imperfections of beginners, he uses the seven deadly sins, applied to the spiritual level—a wonderful exercise for each of us to do. *Beginners in the spiritual life sometimes become proud and complacent in their spiritual success,* like to speak of spiritual matters to others as if they were teachers not learners, and look down on others who they think have not attained the same level of spiritual growth that they have. As their devotion increases, so too does their pride. They compare themselves to others, blind to their own defects and critical of others' weaknesses. They can become consumed with envy of others' progress in the spiritual life, refuse to acknowledge their own failures, and have an intense desire to appear better than they are. These beginners minimize their faults, become discouraged, impatient, and angry at their failings, and long to remove them for the personal satisfaction that would give them. These arrogant know-it-all religious devotees like to receive praise, but never give it.

However, *when beginners are ready to transition to the next level of spiritual growth they see, admit, and reject these weaknesses.* They have true self-knowledge, become humble, think better of others than themselves, and seek to emulate the good they appreciate in others. They focus more on their own inadequacies than their achievements and realize the good they do is always less than they could do. They see good in others and weaknesses in themselves. These beginners who are ready to move along the road to union are always ready to learn from others. They rejoice when others are praised, feeling rather that they are not serving God as well as they ought. They can readily speak of their own failures, and they seek directors who give little praise and a lot of challenge.

Beginners' are often filled with spiritual avarice. Some beginners are never content with the spirit God gives them. They pursue religious objects, experiences, and satisfaction with a possessiveness of heart. They forget that while people can profit from objects and practices of devotion, it is better to focus on love of God and neighbor. These beginners who can become fanatical in their religious devotions and practices will find that it is difficult to purify themselves of attachments without the passive purification of the dark night. But if they do their part, then God will heal them of what they were unable to achieve.

A lot of the imperfections of beginners can be called spiritual lust, not because the lust is spiritual but because it proceeds from spiritual things. They experience reactions similar to lust and impure movements during their spiritual experiences. The gratification that some beginners find in religious devotions and spiritual things inebriates them, fills them with self-assurance in others' presence, and generates an exaggerated pleasure in others' company and appreciation. The dark night places these loves in reasonable order, strengthens love of God, and destroys false loves.

Imperfections of spiritual anger result from the pursuit of spiritual gratification, for when the gratification passes the beginners become irritable, unbearable to others, dejected—all reactions that need to be purified through the dryness of the dark night. Then, through indiscreet zeal these beginners become angry at others' sins and set themselves up as lords of virtue. They become absorbed in one spiritual project or another and angry when others do not share their approach. They also grow angry at their own imperfections in an unhumble impatience, making lots of resolutions but unable to keep them. They lack the patience to wait until God is ready, and this lack of spiritual meekness can only be remedied by the purification of the dark night.

Few beginners avoid the failure of spiritual gluttony due to the delight they find in their spiritual exercises. Focusing more on the spiritual satisfaction than purity and discretion, they go to extremes in their religious practices; penances, fasts, avoiding the guidance of others as they hide their own weakness and excesses from their spiritual guide. These beginners are unreasonable and imperfect; motivated by the pleasure and satisfaction they find in their devotions, they lack submissiveness and any obedience that limits their desire for this accumulation of spiritual practices. They try to make their spiritual director think the way they do, they become sad and testy when they do not get their own way, and they equate serving God with doing what they want.

What they want is to taste and feel God's presence; but this is not God's way and is a serious imperfection and impurity of faith. This defect carries over to their prayer life, where they pursue satisfaction in the devotion, without which they become disconsolate and think they have achieved nothing. These beginners lose the spirit of true devotion and can even abandon prayer when satisfaction is absent, for they are exclusively motivated by the pleasure they find in their devotions. They need spiritual sobriety, temperance, mortification, fear, and submissiveness. They need to learn that perfection is not found in quantity of satisfactions but in knowing how to practice self-denial until God draws them into the dark night.

Beginners also evidence imperfections of spiritual envy and spiritual sloth. These beginners show envy towards the spiritual goods and achievements of others, grieving over others' successes in the spiritual life, resenting when others are praised and they are not. Sloth makes them avoid spiritually challenging exercises and give up practices that do not produce feelings of satisfaction. Seeking such pleasure and delight predominates over self-denial and the pursuit of God's will. They feel an aversion to adapt their will to God's, equating their will and satisfaction with God's will, convinced that what is not their will is not God's will.

Bored with anything that does not produce gratification, they lack the fortitude and effort perfection demands, run away from hardship and the cross, and follow their own whims and satisfactions. The narrow way is saddening and repugnant to them. They cannot actively attain complete mortification of self, so God must accomplish this passively through the dark night; through dryness and darkness God weans them from the imperfections of beginners and moves them to the state of proficients.

Making a serious commitment in love (Passive night of spirit)

Letting God love in us and teach us how to love

We all need God's help to discover authentic love. Left to ourselves we continue with old, immature ways of developing love. Once we allow God to teach us we must be ready for radical changes that are painful to accept for they mean abandoning what we thought was good and setting a new direction. The passive night of spirit deals with the transition from the stage of the proficients to that of union. John describes in detail the nature of this purification and the pain people experience during this transition (see N.2. 4-8). While the night of sense is common and happens to many, "The spiritual night is the lot of very few, those who have been tried and are proficient" (N.1. 8.1). John also points out that God does not normally place a person in the passive night of spirit immediately following that of sense, but rather after many years in the state of proficients with their accompanying serenity and peace (see N.2. 1.1). The description of this night is a profound analysis that shows both John's extensive knowledge of spiritual direction and his own mystical experience.

This struggle for the union of love gives meaning to life. It is the most painful period of the spiritual journey, but the ability to renounce aspects of life that have seemingly been good is a characteristic of authentic love. "[T]he most difficult conquest came about in darkness; but since I was seeking love the leap I made was blind and dark, and I rose so high, so high, that I took the prey" (Poem, "I went out seeking love," verse 2). However, in this night everything around us falls apart and the security we previously had disappears. God no longer seems real, faith loses its challenge, the Church and its teachings seem irrelevant. This dark night becomes a pervasive inner anguish, as a person feels he or she is no longer on firm ground. However, this night is a necessary step on the way to deeper love.

Reflections on the text

In the night of spirit we come face to face with the real, objective picture of life and of ourselves. We become profoundly aware of human creatureliness and finiteness, and intensely conscious of humanity's sinfulness and our own inability to love as we would wish. Nowadays, some spiritualities, focusing on human fulfillment, tend to forget where we have come from and the deep seated failures of the human heart. John does not.

At this stage we now enjoy the serenity that comes with loving contemplation. In dealing with the passive night of spirit John focuses on those who are proficients in the spiritual life. If we reach this stage, we are no longer bound by discursive meditation and the spiritual concerns of beginners. However, total purification is not complete, for the purification of spirit is still lacking. We feel certain needs, aridities, darkness, and conflicts more intensely than in the past. These last for a while but will pass as we return to serenity, and at times God gives some people short experiences of the night followed by serenity. However, those who have the strength and capacity for the prolonged experience can enjoy the delights of God even in the sensory part since that is now purified.

Imperfections of proficients are habitual or actual. Habitual are those imperfections still remaining after the passive night of sense, like deep roots that we have not yet dug out. Habitual imperfections include the natural affections and dullness that results from sin, together with a distracted and inattentive spirit. These too must be illumined, clarified, and recollected by the passive night of spirit in order to ready oneself for deeper love. Actual imperfections occur when we become over-focused on the satisfactions we receive in spiritual communications, beguiled by vain visions and empty prophecies, or drawn by vanity, arrogance, and others' praise. Some people with these imperfections become bold in dealing with God and too secure in their new experiences, just at the point when they were ready to make further progress. They forget that real purification is the work of the spirit.

Proficients are often attracted by the gratification flowing from their spiritual experiences and this helps them be accommodated and united to the spirit, in such a way that they are ready for what lies ahead, but they must let God draw them on. The passive night of senses is just a reformation and bridling of the appetites rather than a full purification. The real purification of the senses begins with the spirit, since all imperfections of the sensory part are rooted in the spirit. In the passive night of spirit both parts are jointly purified; the lower part is purified then strengthened by spiritual support to be strong enough to endure the night ahead; the night that prepares for authentic love.

Welcoming the pain of love

This part of our spiritual journey is painful, but we must welcome the pain of love that comes in the passive night of spirit. Proficients still have actual and habitual imperfections that need to be illumined and purified by the passive night of spirit. With the increased illumination of contemplation a person feels increased affliction and pain at his or her own unworthiness. Such a person, becomes more aware of the awesome otherness of God and recognizes more accurately his or her own failings in the ways of love. In this darkness caused by contemplative illumination one experiences God's absence, feels abandoned and rejected by God, overwhelmed by one's own misery, and it seems one's whole inner self is being torn out. "Although they are aware that they love God, this gives them no consolation, because they think that God does not love them and they are unworthy of his love. Because they see themselves deprived of him and established in their own miseries, they feel they truly bear within themselves every reason for being rejected and abhorred by God" (N.2. 7.7).

At this time we can feel embittered at the loss of past good things and helpless in our inability to think of God as was formerly common. In fact, we enter a period where we fear losing God forever. We discover that God does not act towards us as we thought God would. This shocks us, leaves us empty of previous inadequate knowledge. However, this is God's way of teaching us how different God is from what we thought and how different love must become. This night purifies the intellect of all former ways of understanding, the will of all inordinate affections, and the memory of what stirs affliction, or disturbance, or anticipation of distress, and worry (A.3. 6.3). This prepares us for a new God-given way of knowing in faith, of remembering or anticipating what are greater hopes, and of loving in a new way. Truly, the nights become a deepening of faith, hope, and love, and they bring to a person seeking God a new approach to faith, a new mode of hope, and a new vitality and depth of love.

Reflections on the text

In the passive night of spirit we find ourselves in the presence of the utterly awesome otherness of God. Nothing can take the place of God, and most of our efforts, based as they are on our own limited knowledge, experience, memories, and yearnings, are idols—we make God into our own image and likeness. This has to be purified by the dark night of contemplation in which God is active, removing our false images and giving us a truer picture of who God is for us. The dark night teaches us the values of emptiness. Until we are willing to become empty we cannot be filled with the love God wants to give us. This is painful and John gives us descriptions of this pain.

God challenges us to leave aside old ways of loving. In this journey of faith and love, we must first overcome immature forms of loving before pursuing authentic love. The first stanza of the poem refers to contemplative purification, nakedness, poverty of spirit, and describes how one leaves behind the low means of understanding, the feeble way of loving, and the poor and limited methods of finding satisfaction in God.

> One dark night,
> fired with love's urgent longings

--ah, the sheer grace!—
I went out unseen,
my house being now all stilled

We are now left to journey in darkness to pure faith. We are no longer experiencing former supports, rather now we find ourselves in darkness of the intellect, distress of the will, affliction and anguish of the memory. Thus leaving aside our former way of acting, we are called to God's way. This implies the redirection of the faculties, passions, appetites, and affections exclusively to the love of God. Thus, the intellect moves from human, natural knowing to divine wisdom, the will from its lowly manner of loving to divine love with strength and purity of spirit, the memory from the dead past or falsely imagined future to focus on eternal glory. In this way all our strength and affections are renewed.

Through infused contemplation God teaches us the perfection of love. This contemplation which we receive passively purifies us of habitual ignorance and imperfections and leads to illumination. So, as unpurified persons, we feel affliction and pain. First, because this illumination purifies us by plunging us in our own miseries. The second reason for this pain is our natural, moral, and spiritual weakness before the overwhelming power of God that leads to the feeling of an immense dark load. Oppressed by these burdens, we feel the loss of all past favors and sense that what used to give us support has gone. We should know that God's aim is to grant favors and not chastise, but God's gentle hand certainly feels heavy.

God's interventions make us feel empty at the loss of former immature love. Another kind of pain suffered in the passive night of spirit is that at the sight of our own miseries we feel we are being undone by a cruel spiritual death. God's purifying contemplation so absorbs the human spiritual substance that we feel we are losing ourselves, but this tomb of darkness prepares for a spiritual resurrection. In this suffering we have the conviction that God has abandoned us and cast us into darkness. We experience God's absence, feel chastised and rejected by God, feel unworthy of God and the object of God's anger. Moreover, we also feel forsaken and despised by other people, especially our friends. We also experience an emptiness of all that used to please us whether temporal, natural, or spiritual. We now find ourselves placed in the midst of miseries of imperfections, aridities, emptiness, and abandonment in darkness. It is in this way that contemplation consumes all our affections and imperfect habits, leaving us feeling oppressed, undone, and in inner torment, as the roots of previous imperfections are ripped out.

At this time, we feel we are losing our grip on former ways of love. The afflictions of the will during the dark night are immense, especially when we remember past evils, feel uncertain of any remedy, and think about past spiritual prosperity. We need to have compassion for anyone who suffers in this night, for such a one feels immense suffering and extreme uncertainty about a remedy. But we should also appreciate that, in this very experience, we are being blessed. If this night is to be truly efficacious, it will last for some years, with intervals of illumination, love, and abundant spiritual communication that might even give us the thought that the trials are over. People who are aware of what is happening in their lives will see that something still remains to be done and realize that there is still an enemy within that is just asleep. It is when we feel safe and least expect it that the full force of the purification returns giving the impression to us that we have lost all blessings once again. It now seems to us that we have virtue but are deprived of God and afflicted; aware we love God but feel God no longer loves us. We know we love God but cannot understand why we have no relief, in fact more affliction. We sense we no longer have, nor ever will have, anything deserving of God's love, rather we see clearly the reasons for being rejected by the one we love.

God leaves us feeling helpless in this transition. Since the dark night impedes our faculties we cannot beseech God nor raise our minds and affections to God. Even when we manage to pray it does not seem that God hears. This contemplation deprives us of all natural affections and apprehensions and leaves our spiritual and natural faculties in darkness and emptiness. This happens even though we are unaware of it. Anyone who has gone through this purification finds no satisfaction in anything in particular, but remains in darkness and emptiness, embracing all things in preparation for what lies ahead. Thus purified, we find a facility in perceiving and penetrating even the deep things of God, and an ease in seeing aspects of our own lives that need purifying.

With God's help we find a sense of direction. The brighter the light of contemplation the darker it is to us. But the dark night gives light. The night of contemplation darkens only to illumine, humbles only to exalt, impoverishes and empties so one can enjoy all earthly and heavenly things. Without purification we would be unable to experience the joy of the spirit. In fact, one attachment would be enough to block this experience. The spirit must be totally purified in order to communicate freely in the fullness of the spirit with divine wisdom and enjoy all things.

God guides us to re-focus the three theological virtues on a new love. The dark night purifies the intellect of its natural object and habitual ways of understanding, and this causes great pain. The dark night purifies the will of its former affections and feelings, for the love that is bestowed in divine union exceeds all previous experiences of the will. In dryness and distress we find God's grace removes all previous ways of loving. This, too, is painful for the love of union does not naturally belong to the will, but after the expulsion of all former ways of loving the will is transformed. Only when we are set in emptiness and poverty, purified, and stripped of the old self, can we be ready to live the new life of union with God. The memory too needs to be purified of all previous agreeable and peaceful knowledge and become alien to its usual knowledge and experience. Everything seems strange, as we are made strangers to our previous knowledge and experiences in order to prepare for divine union.

We feel reborn to a new love. We suffer in the dark night so as to be reborn into the life of the spirit by means of the divine inflow. Likewise, we can leave aside all former peace, which was not true peace, for it was both sensory and spiritual, to prepare for a new peace. This passive night of spirit involves many fears, struggles, a sense of being lost, and a feeling that all former blessings have gone. We suffer greatly at the remembrance of our miseries and cry out with profound affliction. We are also filled with doubts and fear that block all sense of hope. We feel torn to shreds. The suffering is so great because what lies ahead is great; so great the end, so great the labor and change. However, the contemplation of itself does not produce pain; rather it is a delightful illumination. The pain results from our weakness, imperfections, inadequate preparation, and qualities that are contrary to the light. Thus we suffer when light illumines our lives.

Appreciating the benefits of true love

"It remains to be said, then, that even though this happy night darkens the spirit, it does so only to impart light concerning all things; and even though it humbles individuals and reveals their miseries, it does so only to exalt them; and even though it impoverishes and empties them of all possessions and natural affections, it does so only that they may reach out divinely to the enjoyment of all earthly and heavenly things, with a general freedom of spirit in them all" (N.2. 9.1). So, this night is a progressive surrender to God and a continuing pursuit of love (see C. 29.10), and a transformation in love (see C. 12.7). The passive night of spirit produces an enkindling of love in the person who then searches for God with impatient love. "Although the soul in her progress does not have the support of any particular interior light of the intellect, or any exterior guide . . . , love alone, which at this period burns by soliciting the heart for the Beloved, is what guides and moves her" (N.2. 25.4).

The three most fundamental energies of the soul are the three theological virtues of faith, hope, and love, gifts of God to transform souls and prepare them for union in love with God. In our days we have many means of spiritual growth available to us. However, it is important to remember that the theological virtues are the divine powers given for our growth, and no others compare to these. These three energies of the soul purify love, teaching us how to think about the One we love, how to remember and hope about this One, and how to bring together every dimension of our love as if nothing else matters.

Reflections on the text

A fruit of the dark night is an intense passion of divine love. The enkindling of love resulting from the passive night of spirit is different from that which results from the passive night of sense, for the latter is in the sensory part whereas this is now in the spiritual part. When we are in the midst of these trials we do not understand anything particular for the intellect is in darkness, but we experience being transformed by a strong divine love. At first we become aware of the power of this love, but do not possess it, still remaining in darkness and doubt. However, we long for this love and find no rest or satisfaction. Rather, this suffering unaccompanied by certain hope leads us to intensified anxiety and affliction. Thus, we long for God with the desire and anxiety of love. While in this darkness, we still experience a certain companionship and interior strength, and when the darkness passes we feel alone, empty, and weak. This union of the will and the intellect and the resulting enkindling of love is a delightful experience and a beginning of the experience of union in love.

In the passive night of spirit we are immersed in the deeper longings of love. The dark night of contemplation at times leads to the burning of the will in love, at other times it illumines the soul and communicates mystical knowledge to the intellect, even though the will remains in dryness. This thirst of love is different from that experienced in the night of senses. It is far greater and is felt in the higher, spiritual part, even though the sensory part can participate somewhat in the experience. But, the longing of the spirit is greater for it is aware of an immense and incomparable good that it lacks, and intense suffering results.

In this experience of love we feel everything seems possible. At this point in the experience of the night we long for God and feel we have lost God or been abandoned by God. This causes fear, for we could endure this suffering if only we knew there was nothing to fear and that God was pleased with our efforts. In other words we have the love of esteem for God. When later the fire of love comes on top of this esteeming love we acquire strength, courage, boldness, and longing. This love inebriates us and fills us with courage.

This is a time when we discover how to love authentically. At this point we rise up and anxiously go in search of God. This love develops in four phases: 1. Longing love (impatient), 2. Esteeming love (intense, but not passionate), 3. Burning love (passionate), 4. Perfect love (union). Immersed in darkness, a person experiences the absence of God, and is filled with impatient love. Although feeling unworthy of God, we still possess a bold energy to go and find God and be in union. This love imparts a force to love authentically, and authentic love implies union and so we seek it. However, the intellect is still in darkness, and we continue to see our own weaknesses and feel unworthy. As was said above, darkness is not caused by the light but by our imperfections, so at first we still only feel darkness and evil. After purification is complete we see clearly our immense benefits and goods, when the intellect is illumined with supernatural light, the will informed by love, and the memory changed by divine conversion.

Now we find ourselves free from false loves. The enamored soul must leave the security of the house to reach the goal, and so he or she goes out at night when all operations, passions and appetites are asleep, for union is not possible when they are active. In the purification of the dark night, God puts to sleep all these faculties, passions, affections, and appetites, so one can go out to the union of love. What a fortunate experience to be free of the control of senses, such can only be understood by one who has experienced it, and can now understand how the life of the spirit is true freedom.

Understanding the characteristics of authentic spiritual love

Journeying in this passive night of spirit, the soul finds security through the dark contemplation that is infused in a person through love. In time a person begins to feel caught up in this love and to consider all else as insignificant, and then comes to experience "the inebriation and courage of love" (N.2. 13.6). As we shall see later, John presents ten steps on a ladder of love that leads to union with God. But the goal is not just union for it also implies the total renewal of self. One's humanity is not destroyed in the nights, rather it reaches its full potential. A person then re-finds all values of life in God. What was a dark night becomes "the tranquil night at the time of the rising dawn" (C. 15). John describes the beauty and thrill of this resulting life of union in the *Spiritual Canticle* and the *Living Flame of Love*.

Reflections on the text

God prepares us to love well. The night of the spirit gives us the experience of the horror of being unable to love and of being convinced of being unloved and unlovable. Then it prepares us to love well; to feel the absence of One who is loved, to feel unworthy when in that presence, to long to be with the One who is loved, and want to sacrifice everything for that loving presence. The night of spirit shows us that when we love someone deeply, we give the Beloved a special place in our mind as knowledge gives way to faith. We also give the Beloved a special place in our memories— knowing that lovers hope more than remember. Then, we give the Beloved a special place in our hearts reserved exclusively for this One. All the trials of the dark night do not lead to the risk of being lost; rather we are saved in this dark night. Each one of us, departing by a living faith, escapes securely and finds greater safety because all our affections are mortified and purified.

We find security in the dark night for when the appetites are purified we are freed from any error caused by them, liberated from our own failings and from the three great enemies of the world, evil, and flesh. So when we walk in darkness and emptiness, we walk securely, for when evils are impeded, only the good of union with God is imparted to the appetites and faculties. When we feel darkened, dry, and incapacitated we should rejoice, because when God takes our hands through the darkness our own actions will be purified. We are advancing securely because we are lost to what we knew and tasted, and going by a way neither tasted nor known. Another reason for this sense of security is that we advance by suffering with the strength God gives, and it is in suffering that virtues are practiced and acquired and we are purified, made wiser, and become more cautious. A further reason why we walk securely in this darkness is that the light of contemplation so absorbs us that we are protected and freed from all that is not God, since God causes one to lose all appetite for anything else. Thus, contemplation brings us closer to God, in security and loving care. Yet another reason for security is that God bestows fortitude so that we become determined not to commit offenses against God, and not to omit anything that could be of service. This enkindling of love fills us with vigilant care and solicitude for the things of God, paying homage to God and withdrawing appetites from all else.

Contemplation is not only dark but it is secret. Dark contemplation is secret because it is mystical theology communicated and infused into us through love. This infused communication is secret to the intellect and other faculties. The purifying contemplation is hidden because the illumination transcends everything sensory and is ineffable. So, we have no way of expressing its meaning, or form an image to explain it to others, even to spiritual directors. Rather, each one feels quiet, content, aware of God, and convinced all goes well. This mystical wisdom can also be called secret because it engulfs and hides us within itself, removed from all else. We feel caught up in this love and understand how base all else is. A final reason this contemplation can be called secret is that it is the way that God guides us to union through unknowing, since these experiences are not known humanly. God's illumination causes darkness, and the way to God is hidden, not appreciated while being sought but only when already found. This secret wisdom is also like a ladder of ten steps to divine love and we shall discuss this elsewhere.

When we journey in this night we also seem to be "disguised" in white, green, and red; white for faith, green for hope, and red for charity. The pure whiteness of faith blinds the intellect against evil and obtains the favor of the Beloved. Green signifies hope that gives courage and strength and raises a person to things of eternal life. With hope we never set store by anything of this world, but live only in the hope of eternal life. No one can pursue the goal of love without unrelenting hope. Thus, people advance through this dark night and secret night in the disguise of hope, empty of all possessions and supports. The perfection of the disguise is the red toga of charity which adds elegance to faith and hope and brings us closer to pleasing God. This charity protects us and strengthens and invigorates all other virtues. Where true love is present, we leave aside all other loves and advance to perfect union with God. These three parts of our disguise prepare the faculties for union with God. Faith darkens and empties the intellect, hope empties and withdraws the memory from satisfaction in all created things, charity empties and purifies the affections and appetites of the will of everything that is not God—thus leading to union.

John comments on line three and concludes his explanation of stanza two. *It is a great grace for us to undertake this departure,* thus liberating ourselves from the influences of evil, the world, and one's own sensuality. In this way we reach freedom of spirit, becoming heavenly instead of earthly, divine instead of human. John feels he has adequately described the night and its resulting blessings.

> In darkness, and secure,
> by a secret ladder disguised,
> --ah, the sheer grace!—
> In darkness and concealment,
> My house being now all stilled.

The fourth line of the poem gives *a description of the soul's hiding place*. "In concealment" refers to the security experienced at this time, when we walk in darkness, hidden from evil. Infused contemplation frees and hides the soul, for it is infused passively without the use of the exterior and interior faculties of the sensory part of a person, and thus free from any obstacles these faculties can cause. In this darkness there is more room for spiritual communication without hindrance from the sensory part or the temptations of evil. When we struggle through this period, greater graces are granted directly by God, greater than all previous blessings, bringing delight and peace unhindered by the sensory part. No one attains these blessings without total nakedness and purification in darkness and concealment. At this point we become totally spiritual in the highest degree of prayer and intimacy with God, passions and appetites are eliminated, "my house being now all stilled."

Through God's influence we obtain habitually perfect rest and quietude. Since the superior part of the soul is now, like the lower, at rest in appetites and faculties, we go to divine union with God through love, with peace in both sensory and spiritual parts. We are now touched by the divinity, thus purified, quieted, strengthened, and made stable to receive permanently divine union. When thus united to God, we find a new bond in the possession of love. We cannot reach this union without remarkable purity which has been attained by vigorous mortification and detachment from all creatures which is the radical work of God in the soul.

In the third stanza we find how *a person enumerates and extols the good properties of the night*, by which he or she has obtained the desired goal of security.

On that glad night,
In secret, for no one saw me,
Nor did I look at anything,
With no other light or guide
Than the one that burned in my heart.

First property, having been led by a solitary and secret contemplation nothing pertaining to senses can any longer detain the soul on this journey to union. Second property, the person is free of all hindrance from forms and figures of natural apprehensions in the faculties that usually prevent him or her from being united with God. Third property, love alone is what guides and moves an individual; one has no support of any particular interior light of intellect and no guide. Deprived of all satisfactions in dense darkness the individual soars to God in an unknown way along the road of solitude, on that glad night where the love that was sought throughout the journey is now achieved.

In the book of the *Dark Night* John explains the various stages in the development of the spiritual journey to union in love. John would also be the first to acknowledge that life is more complex than a scheme, and the process described is not completely regular nor the same for everyone. So, while no one wants to impose a scheme on anyone, it is useful to have a general feel for the movement of the spiritual life and key experiences that occur during the progress, and John gives us this with extraordinary clarity. Certainly, there is only one way to God and that is to follow Jesus whose love led him to the cross. The experience of the cross comes in a special way in the nights.

As we move through the nights "fired by love's urgent longings," we must face up to the crazy pain of love. In letters John wrote to Doña Juana de Pedraza (L. 11, 19) he seems to be speaking to us all. At times we seem to be experiencing some of the "grief, afflictions, and loneliness" of the night. John reminds us "they are knocks and rappings at the door of your soul so it might love more." He acknowledges supportively the pain we feel and tells us, "it behooves us not to go without the cross, just as our Beloved did not go without it, even to the death of love." When we walk in "these darknesses and voids of spiritual poverty," we should not worry for nothing is failing us. Rather John tells us "Do not worry, but be glad." "You were never better off than now," "God does one a great favor when he darkens the faculties and impoverishes the soul." "God is leading you by a road most suitable for you." "Desire no other path than this." Thus, for John the experiences of the dark night are one proof of God's loving interventions in our lives. The night is essential to growth, for growth takes place in transitions and crises. This darkness is a test of love which we must undergo in confidence, patience, and ever deeper faith.

Chapter 6
Immersion in the mystery of love

Reflections on the Living Flame of Love

United in love with the Holy Spirit

Immersed in the life and love of the Holy Trinity

Transformed by God's love and attributes

Understanding the cosmos in union with the love of the world

When we commit ourselves to journey to union with God in love we will find we are assisted in our journey by the Living Flame of Love. The Living Flame, who is none other than the Holy Spirit, accompanies us at every stage of the journey. In the early stages, when we enter contemplation, the Living Flame purifies our imperfections in order to prepare us for the inflow of God's love and for the transformation that will come later. At this time the Living Flame causes us pain and allows us to feel dryness, darkness, distress, and lack of self-knowledge. It is a time of trials for our intellect, memory, and will. So, the Flame is oppressive in its purifying and illuminating actions but later becomes our guide in the maturing of love.

The book, the *Living Flame of Love,* goes beyond the early stages in the spiritual life and describes the final step in a vision of love. It describes the end of a journey that began in the purifying longings of love. The person in his or her journey then passed through a period of illumination regarding the God of love and his or her own need of love. Then the person reached the early stage of union in spiritual betrothal. *The Living Flame of Love* picks up from the final stage of union in the love of spiritual marriage and describes, in great beauty, several aspects of this final stage in the union of love. All these ideas are part of John's wonderful vision of love.

Introduction

The commentary on the *Living Flame* describes the depth of the love relationship in the later stages in the spiritual life, often referred to as spiritual marriage. This relationship is between a lover who seeks union with God and God the primary Lover. "[T]hese stanzas treat of a love deeper in quality and more perfect within this very state of transformation" (F. Prologue.3). It is different from the *Spiritual Canticle*, even though close in time and, to some extent, in thought. It describes situations outside our normal understanding of the stages in the spiritual life, while insisting that what it describes is not itself a stage, but rather four facets of the final encounter of spiritual marriage. The *Spiritual Canticle* emphasizes the role of Christ in the maturing of love in the journey to divine union, whereas the *Living Flame* emphasizes the role of the Holy Spirit as agent and guide of all the work of Christian holiness. In his earlier works John of the Cross describes the purification and dismantling of a false self, false values, false loves, and false understanding and focus of the intellect, will, and memory. Then in the *Spiritual Canticle* he presents the journey of two lovers to union. Now, in the *Living Flame* he looks at four aspects of the singular union achieved at the end of the *Spiritual Canticle*. First, he describes how a person is united in love with the Holy Spirit. Second, he stresses how a person is immersed in the life and love of the Holy Trinity. Third, he comments on how one is transformed by God's love and attributes. Finally, he shows how in spiritual marriage one understands the whole cosmos in union with the love of the Word. The *Living Flame* does not offer norms and guidance to get to the end, but rather, describes the nature of the end and clarifies the meaning of human existence and the call of humanity to transformation in union with God.

The "Living Flame" is the shortest of John's major poems—just twenty four lines in comparison to the forty lines of the "Dark Night," and two hundred in the final version of the "Spiritual Canticle." Although the poem is short, John seems on fire with his subject, and Fr. Gabriel calls the commentary "a book of fire." While John's other works consider the spiritual journey and the means one should employ or accept at various stages, the *Living Flame* in both poem and commentary considers the end of the journey, the goal. In every sense the *Living Flame* is the peak of John's teaching. Unlike the *Spiritual Canticle* and the *Ascent-Dark Night* that are full of movement and progress, the *Living Flame* is not developmental and can seem static in comparison to the others. It presents a succession of parallel scenes without progress. However, it is filled with the tension and satisfaction of love and gives a deeper understanding and development of the love of encounter and union.

United in love with the Holy Spirit

In the stage of spiritual marriage which John of the Cross describes in the *Living Flame of Love*, the living flame is the Holy Spirit who in this stanza is a fire that consumes, transforms, and enflames the lover who seeks God. Such a one, transformed in love, feels the activity of the Holy Spirit in two ways—as a permanent presence of transforming love and as an experience of enflamed love in the Spirit's acts within the person. The former is a habit of love, the latter an act of intense love that is an effect of the habit.

This union of love takes place in the very depths of the human spirit. There, in the transformed interior of a person who seeks God, God does everything, without the person doing anything except to receive from God. God works in the depths of such a person, in his or her very center, so that all activities become divine. Thus, the Holy Spirit enflames the purified seeker and transforms him or her in love by means of extraordinary communications. The person rejoices in this fullness of communication and perfection and is absorbed in God.

In this state of spiritual marriage and fullness of love, the spiritual person longs for a union that can only be achieved beyond this life, for he or she still feels incompleteness and yearns for the fullness of love the Lord alone brings. However, the lover no longer experiences pain in this longing, for more than anything else he or she finds joy in fulfilling God's will. Moreover, the Living Flame enflames the seeker with acts of love so intense that he or she cannot help looking ahead to the fullness of union that is only now glimpsed. The Holy Spirit rouses and invites this person to maintain a focus on what lies ahead.

The lover can only reach the next step of union through death which is not painful, but a sweet and powerful encounter of love. He or she is ready for union with God, feels richly endowed by God, and is aware that nothing is now lacking except to break through this final veil and leave behind the entanglements of this life. Transformation from this life to the next results from a strong and impetuous touch of love. It is an intense act in a short time, done without any long immediate preparation. The lover wants no further delay and, moved by the force of love, begs that the veil of life be torn immediately. So, this first stanza describes the role of the Spirit in this transformation in love. It is an encounter in which God undertakes to purify, perfect, penetrate, and absorb a person in God. It is an encounter that is more delightful than all others.

Reflections on stanza one

The first stanza of the *Living Flame of Love* describes how we are united in love with the Holy Spirit, feel completely transformed, possessed by God, inflamed in divine union, and close to the union of eternity. The person in the poem asks that the Holy Spirit remove the last obstacle to total union.

> O living flame of love
> that tenderly wounds my soul
> in its deepest center! Since
> now you are not oppressive,
> now consummate! If it be your will:
> tear through the veil of this sweet encounter!

So, this first stanza of the *Living Flame* describes the goal of contemplative life, namely union with God in love. *This transformation in God is achieved by the Living Flame, who is the Holy Spirit.* The stanza recognizes the abundance of God's love and gifts in the experience of spiritual marriage, it looks back to former times in a digression, and towards the end of the stanza it anxiously launches out to the goal of total union in eternity. A person who enters this experience feels on fire with the love of God and experiences in the depths of being that he or she is enflamed with the love of God. This love of union is not acquired, it is given. The Flame of Love transforms and totally possesses the lover of God so profoundly that he or she feels that there is no further goal in this life. This experience is a complete fusion of the activities of the person with those of the Holy Spirit.

The lover in the poem feels the Holy Spirit in two ways—as a fire which consumes and transforms, and as a fire that burns and flares up within one's inner spirit. So, there is a situation of transformation which is a permanent habit of life, and there are further moments, acts of love, when the Holy Spirit overwhelms the seeker's will with sublime love. The person now experiences union of wills, of hearts, of actions in conformity with God's, and of service and love of others. At this time the involvement of the Holy Spirit is so powerful that the lover no longer acts on his or her own. Rather the Holy Spirit takes over the individual's acts, making them God's acts. The Holy Spirit moves the soul in all its actions— however they are still the person's actions, for the Holy Spirit moves one to do them. This experience is so transforming for anyone, "it makes the soul live in God spiritually and experience the life of God" (F. 1.6). This enjoyment of God in a living way is a foretaste of eternity.

The spiritual person who seeks union with God is now motivated by the will of God in everything. The Living Flame's transformation takes place in the deepest center of such a person, where one dwells with God, loving and enjoying God with his or her entire being and with every act, work, and inclination. When love permeates every aspect of a person's life, strength, and power, he or she can enter into God and center life on God alone. The stronger the love, the deeper will be the union. The more a person is transformed and concentrated in God the more intense, tender, stronger, and substantial is a person's delight. Granting these extraordinary blessings is part of the strategy of a generous and loving God who wants to dwell in anyone who has prepared for these gifts

At this point in the *Living Flame a lover thinks and wants what God thinks and wants.* He or she longs for the consummation of spiritual marriage. Although conformed to the will of God and transformed by love, the seeker still feels empty and lives in hope for the total completion of love that still lies ahead. This longing is no longer painful; it is love that longs for deeper love. Now, "love is the friend of the power of love" (F. 1.33). Having broken through the temporal veil of attraction to creatures, and the natural veil of inclinations and actions—both resulting from renunciation and purification, the lover now wants to break through the third veil, the sensitive one that keeps him or her bound to this life. At this point, the spiritual seeker longs for death, feels overwhelmed with the gifts and blessings received from God, and is ready to pass beyond the last veil. "God permits it in this state to discern its beauty and He entrusts to it the gifts and virtues he has bestowed, for everything is converted into love and praises" (F. 1. 31). A person at this point perceives the power of the next life, views everything as God does: "All things are nothing to it, and it is nothing in its own eyes; God alone is its all" (F. 1.32). The force of love that such a person feels at this time makes him or her want to suffer no further delay in passing beyond this final veil of life. Having given oneself to love in this life, there is readiness for the final encounter.

The *Living Flame* describes how the Holy Spirit makes a person live in God. This transformation in the depths of one's personality is *an encounter with the mystery of God that gives one a new source of identity and destiny*. In this poem and commentary, the individual is on fire with love, inflamed in divine union, immersed in the revelations of the Trinity, and so gifted that only a veil separates him or her from complete union. Of course, no one earns this. It is God who draws us to divine life, for God always takes the initiative, being the primary Lover. It is the nature of God to be love and to love. Always moved by infinite love, it is of the essence of God to extend love—it is who God is. Salvation history describes God's strategy of love for us all, and it tells us how God constantly takes a risk with us, sharing and inviting us to love.

The Living Flame challenges us to think about human existence in a different way. God desires to share divine life with us, to communicate a new way of living and loving, and to establish an intimate relationship with each of us. We are called to live the life of God. If we can only remove obstacles to God's actions within us, then God is free to transform us into who we are intended to be, who we were created to be. The psalmist reminds us that this steadfast love of God is precious, it is better than any other aspect of life (Ps 63.3). This transforming love of the Holy Spirit in this Living Flame gladdens a person's heart and allows him or her to enjoy "the glory of God's glory in likeness and shadow" (F. 3.16). The seeker now possesses God in love and is possessed by God's love.

Immersed in the life and love of the Holy Trinity

In the second stanza of the *Living Flame* we read how the Holy Spirit, working in one who seeks love, purifies and enflames according to the divine will and to each one's preparations. The Holy Spirit's communications of love are very strong and enflame a person in such a way that he or she become a burning fire for others. While this flame of love purifies, it does not consume, destroy, or afflict the person. Rather, it divinizes, and delights, as it burns gently. People who receive this communication find delight and satisfaction in its affliction. This experience is truly a contemplative communication of the divinity, who heals by wounding with love. So, this Flame of Love strengthens, empowers, and imbues a person with love. Since the burning wound is so wonderful, the lover realizes how wonderful also must be the one who causes it.

The gentle and loving hand of the Father touches the spiritual person, wounding but bringing life and healing. Refined, cleansed, purified, and withdrawn from every creature, the lover of God is now ready to receive the Word, the Son of the Father, immense and delicate. The more abundantly the delicate touch pervades such a person, the purer he or she becomes. The delicate communication is indescribable and simple without form or figure. It is produced in the person by the infinite being of God who touches subtly, lovingly, eminently, and delicately. This touch is not yet perfect but anticipates eternal life. Sometimes, this experience of the touch of the Holy Spirit overflows to the body and sensory part. Thus, the body through this unction or anointing participates in the delights of the soul.

There are two kinds of complete union in life. The one we are accustomed to consists in the vision of God attained by natural death. But there is a second one that is perfect spiritual life acquired through purification, for without mortification one cannot attain the perfection of the spiritual life of union with God. In the new life, spiritual faculties (intellect, will, and memory) are focused on God and appetites and activities become divine. A person thus transformed lives the life of God and has changed from death to spiritual life. The intellect becomes one with God's intellect. God's will and a person's will are now one. The memory no longer perceives the figures of creatures but is united to the mind and future of God. Natural appetites that used to relish creatures now find fulfillment in God alone. All movements and operations of an individual are now dead to their former life and alive to God and moved by the Holy Spirit. So he or she becomes God through participation—dead to all he or she used to be and alive to what God is.

Reflections on stanza two

The second stanza of the poem proclaims that it is the Holy Trinity who effects the divine work of union. The Holy Spirit is a powerful fire of infinite love that transforms a person into itself. The gentle hand refers to the Father, generous and powerful, always ready to bestow gifts on those who seek him. The only begotten Son of the Father is the delicate touch that wounds to bring this healing love.

> O sweet cautery,
> O delightful wound!
> O gentle hand! O delicate touch
> that tastes of eternal life
> and pays every debt!
> In killing you changed death to life.

Part of the experience of spiritual marriage is *the transforming work of the Holy Trinity indwelling in those who reach this state.* This experience is of all three working together as one, and yet it seems that each one of the Trinity has a particular role to play. The Holy Spirit cauterizes the lover with a delightful wound.

The Son shares a delicate touch that gives a taste of eternal life. The Father transforms the person with a gentle hand that pays all former debts. This transformation is the efficacious gift of the Trinity and the person looks with gratitude at both the gift and the Giver.

The Holy Spirit transforms a person by touching him or her with the fire of love that is so intense it cauterizes the soul, burning away imperfections and transforming the person into a burning flame. Here in the poem the cauterizing flame does not afflict but divinizes and delights. The flame does not weary or restrict the lover but enlarges and enriches him or her. Other effects of this cauterizing include communications, personal satisfaction, and fulfillment. This cauterizing causes a delightful wound of love. When someone receives a burn he or she needs medicine to cure it, but this burning is the medicine; the more it wounds the more it cures and heals. Thus the seeker of love becomes healthy in love and transformed in love. The Holy Spirit produces this cauterizing activity in order to bring delight and joy according to the capacity of each one.

The merciful and omnipotent Father treats each one with a gentle hand. Human beings express themselves through their bodies and the gentle hand can heal, calm, console, encourage, sympathize, and support. It is very special that John sees the Father treating us in this way. Although nations tremble before the power of God, God treats each one with extraordinary gentleness. "You are friendly and gentle with me, how much more lovingly, graciously, and gently do You permanently touch my soul!" (F. 2.16). This gentle hand causes death and gives life. "You have wounded me in order to cure me, O divine hand, and you have put to death in me what made me lifeless, deprived me of God's life in which I now see myself live" (F. 2.16).

Although terrible and strong, *the Son touches a lover with gentleness when he is permanently hidden within a person who is refined, cleansed, and purified.* The delicate touch is brought by the Word, the Son of God, who penetrates a person's very substance transforming him or her in God. Thus, the Son withdraws the lover from all other interests to focus on himself alone, pervading the person's very substance. "O Word, indescribably delicate touch, produced in the soul only by Your most simple being, which, since it is infinite, is infinitely delicate and hence touches so subtly, lovingly, eminently, and delicately!" (F. 2.20). This touch is so special that it gives a taste of eternal life, as inexpressibly profound as is possible in this life. "As a result the soul tastes here all the things of God, since God communicates to it fortitude, wisdom, love, beauty, grace, and goodness, etc. Because God is all these things, a person enjoys them in only one touch of God, and the soul rejoices within its faculties and within its substance" (F. 2.21). This experience can be so deep that it overflows into the body that then shares in these delights.

John's mysticism is eminently Trinitarian. This is his distinctive way of speaking about God and of explaining our participation in divine life. While John's focus on the Trinity permeates the entire poem and commentary, it is particularly pronounced in stanza two. There are two kinds of life; that which comes after death and consists in the vision of God, and that which comes in this life from purification that leads to the possession of God in the union of love. In this latter case, a person brings death to the old life, and through union with God he or she lives the life of God. Such a lover has passed from death to a new spiritual life. This happens when the intellect is moved and formed by faith, the will changed into a life of divine love, the memory changed into possession of God in a vision of hope, and the appetites changed so that they now delight in God alone. Every aspect of one's being is now alive to God. "Accordingly, the intellect of this soul is God's intellect; its will is God's will; its memory is the memory of God; its delight is God's delight" (F. 2.34). The seeker has now become God through participation. He or she is dead to former life and alive to God who continually renews all things. Such a one rejoices in this new life, grateful to God who has wrought this transformation by changing death into life.

The second stanza of the *Living Flame* emphasizes how *the Trinity transforms into itself the person it touches, changing every aspect of death into life*. Thus John comments on a person's reactions to such grace; "you cause death and you give life" (F. 2.16), and "you put to death in me what made me lifeless" (F. 2.16). The whole of the spiritual journey is a movement from death to life; in fact, God uses death to gain life. The death that the Trinity brings about concerns old ways of thinking, possessing, and loving. "Let it be known that what the soul calls death is all that goes to make up the old man: the entire engagement of the faculties (memory, intellect, and will) in the things of the world . . . . All this is the activity of the old life, which is death to the new life of the spirit" (F. 2.33).

However, the indwelling of *the Holy Trinity transforms the three great spiritual faculties*. "The Blessed Trinity inhabits the soul by divinely illuminating its intellect with the wisdom of the Son, delighting its will in the Holy Spirit, and by absorbing it powerfully and mightily in the unfathomed embrace of the Father's sweetness" (F. 1.15). John says the Trinity achieves this by acting in the strength of love as a cautery, a delicate touch, and a gentle hand—all changing death to life (F. 2.1). In this way the Trinity converts a lover into a fire of love. Of this transformation each person can say, "You have put to death in me what made me lifeless, deprived me of God's life in which I now see myself live. You granted this with the liberality of your generous grace" (F. 2.16). The *Living Flame* tells us how all this is done by the Trinity's transforming love. John quotes an interesting verse from the prophet Hosea: "O death, I will be your death" (Hosea 13.14). Thus, God absorbs the seeker in a life of love.

Transformed by God's love and attributes

God reveals the divine self to spiritual seekers by means of the divine attributes. These become like many lamps in a person's heart, each one distinctly and all of them together giving knowledge and enflaming him or her in love. God's omnipotence becomes a lamp of omnipotence, sharing and bestowing all knowledge. God as wisdom becomes a lamp of wisdom within each one. Likewise, the divine attributes of goodness, justice, fortitude, mercy, and all others, communicate light and envelop a person in love, so he or she experiences all these attributes vitally. A person who longs for God delights in this experience, as each lamp burns in love and enlightens and enflames all the other lamps. Thus, the person enjoys all attributes together, and each one separately, but always enriched by all the others. Absorbed in the love of these attributes, a person becomes more alive in love and perceives that love is the essential aspect of eternal life. So, the lover experiences that God is wise and loves with wisdom, is infinitely good and loves with goodness, is holy and with holiness loves. So, God loves the person with the full power of all the divine attributes—loving with justice, mercy, liberality, absolute humility, and so on. In this way God reveals and communicates the divine self in this union, while a person is transformed through participation in God and in God's attributes.

In preparation for union with God in spiritual marriage God anoints the faculties—intellect, will, and memory—but the suffering that is part of the experience can be intense. Anointing means setting aside someone or something for a special purpose or function. So, we anoint kings, and priests, and even some of the symbols of their office. We want God to anoint our spiritual faculties so that our intellect, memory, and will are set aside to be focused exclusively on God and enable us to know, possess, and love God in an exclusive way. At that time the satisfaction, fullness, and delight of the faculties will be great when they are transformed by the possession of divine knowledge, love, and glory. Through his or her three faculties a person experiences and enjoys the objects of the spiritual faculties, the grandeurs of God's wisdom and excellence. Through these deep caverns of feeling (the faculties) a spiritual person has power and capacity for experiencing, possessing, and tasting the deep knowledge and splendors of the attributes of God.

A person such as the one in the poem enjoys fullness in the union of the intellect and affection with God and surrenders totally to God in wonderful ways. Concerning love, first, the person loves God not through himself or herself but through God, loving through the Holy Spirit as the Father and the Son love each other. Second, he or she also loves God in God, for he or she is now absorbed in God. Third, the person loves God on account of who God is—not because God is generous or glorious, but because God is all this in essence. Regarding fruition and fullness, the lover now enjoys God by means of God, since its intellect is now united to all the attributes of God. Second, he or she enjoys God directly without intermingling of creatures. Third, the lover of God enjoys God because of who God is in the divine self without seeking pleasure for itself. The person praises God excellently. First, seeing it as a duty, second, for the gifts received, and third because of who God is without any thought of benefit. The person expresses the excellence of gratitude: first, for all natural and spiritual goods received, second, because of finding great delight in praising God, and third, because of who God is.

Reflections on stanza three

This third stanza of the poem describes how the seeker of union is immersed in the life and love of the Holy Trinity. God discloses the divine life to a person in descriptors or attributes which become like lamps giving light and heat. God is all these attributes in simple oneness of being, and an individual experiences these attributes in one simple act of union.

O lamps of fire!
in whose splendors
the deep caverns of feeling,
once obscure and blind,
now give forth, so rarely, so exquisitely,
both warmth and light to their Beloved.

The first stanza celebrates how the Holy Spirit transforms in the deepest center of being the individual who reaches spiritual marriage. The second stanza proclaims that the experience of spiritual marriage is the transforming work of the Holy Trinity; the Holy Spirit cauterizes with a delightful wound, the Son shares a delicate touch that gives a taste of eternal life, and the Father transforms with a gentle hand that pays all former debts. This third stanza rejoices in the fact that the *person receives abundant and lofty knowledge of God, communications of light and love to the three spiritual faculties of intellect, memory, and will.* This communication is so illumined and filled with love that the person who strives to journey to God becomes a source of light and love for others. Appreciating these gifts, we sing of this new transformed life that has been received.

No one can know God fully in this life, but *we try to appreciate the divine life by means of a series of descriptors or attributes.* John suggests we vitally participate in these attributes. "God in His unique and simple being is all the powers and grandeurs of His attributes" (F. 3.2). In the transformation described in this stanza, God communicates this knowledge to those who seek divine love—that God is each of these qualities distinctly and all of them together in simple oneness of being. This communication is so transformative for us, that we become these attributes in union with God. "We deduce that the soul, like God, gives forth light and warmth through each of these innumerable attributes. Each of these attributes is a lamp which enlightens it and transmits the warmth of love" (F. 3. 2).

John calls each of these attributes a lamp of fire because lamps give both light and heat, and *each of these attributes of God gives illumination and love to the person seeking loving union*. Thus, when God communicates divine omnipotence to an individual, he or she knows that omnipotence and love go together. When God communicates wisdom, God "grants the soul light and the warmth of the love of God according to His wisdom" (F. 3.3). Likewise God communicates all the other divine attributes. This is not simply intellectual knowledge of God but living, vivifying, and vital knowledge. Each person does not just know this about God but experiences it.

Moreover, *the lover's experience is not just of each one separately but of all together at the same time, each one influencing all the others*. "Each lamp burns in love, and the warmth from each furthers the warmth of the other, and the flame of one, the flame of the other, just as the light of one sheds light on the other, because through each attribute the other is known" (F. 3.5). The communication of the vital interrelationship of all these attributes is wonderful. They are not just illuminating but loving, and "the soul perceives clearly that love is proper to eternal life" (F. 3.5).

Each one loves and does good according to his or her nature. God loves us with omnipotence, wisdom, mercy, justice, and so on; *God loves with the full force of all the divine attributes*. God is omnipotent and loves us omnipotently, God is holy and loves with holiness, God is truth and loves with truthfulness, and so on. God's communications are like lamps of fire, bringing light and warmth. They are also like living waters of the spirit that refresh and satisfy thirst. John concludes this section; "Everything can be expressed in this statement: The soul becomes God from God through participation in him and in his attributes, which it terms the 'lamps of fire'" (F. 3.8).

John calls the divine attributes "lamps of fire", but he also thinks of them as "overshadowings," since *they cast a shadow of protection, favor, and grace over those who seek God*. Each divine attribute casts a shadow of itself; divine wisdom casts a shadow of wisdom on the person, God's beauty casts a protective shadow of beauty over us, God's infinite goodness casts a grace-filled goodness on the lover, and so on. It is extraordinary to see the awesome generosity of God in the gifts bestowed on those in this spiritual state described in the third stanza.

In this profound divine communication the spiritual faculties of intellect, memory, and will are transformed. John calls these faculties "the deep caverns of feeling" for it is through them that a person experiences and enjoys the revelation of divine communication in the attributes. Prior to God's enlightenment and illumination these faculties were "once obscure and blind." God illumines the faculties through the vital communication of divine attributes; this is entirely gift, something the faculties could never have attained on their own. Previously, the faculties responded like a person who has a cataract over the eye, never seeing things clearly, but rather pursuing objects they thought were important although they never were. Once the spiritual faculties have been illumined by communication of the divine attributes, they surrender to a new purpose—to give back the light and heat they have received. The intellect is now united to God's intellect, the will is united to God's goodness and gives back that same goodness to God. "And according to the excellence of the divine attributes (fortitude, beauty, justice, etc.), which the Beloved communicates, is the excellence with which the soul's feelings give joyfully to Him the very light and heat it receives from Him" (F. 3.78). Thus, the person in this state is one with God and God through participation—the intellect of the two is one intellect, the will of the two is one will, and the memory of the two is one vision of life, and God's operation and the lover's become one.

At this point one rejoices in being able to give back to God something of his or her own; *"giving all that was given it by Him in order to repay love"* (F. 3.79). This reciprocal gift of love and total mutual surrender is part of the spiritual marriage described in these stanzas. "This is the soul's deep satisfaction and happiness: to see that it gives to God more than in itself it is worth" (F. 3.80). The spiritual faculties are transformed and surrender themselves to God in renewed love, fulfillment, praise, and gratitude.

Understanding the cosmos in union with the love of the word

As we search for divine union we address God with deep love, thanking God for the effects already produced from this union, namely an awakening of one's spirit in gentleness and love and the breathing of God in us. So, the spiritual seeker experiences an awakening of love in the very center and depths of his or her being, and feels so captivated and aroused in love that it seems the whole world participates in this intense movement of love. In this experience a lover sees the beauty of everything in the world, and he or she appreciates how all creatures find their life and strength in God. Here is the delight of this awakening: the spiritual seeker knows creatures through God and not God through creatures. God reveals to the lover who seeks greater love the divine life and being and the harmony of every creature in that divine life. So, such a person sees God in essence and God in relationship to all the creatures of the world. Through this cosmic awakening, a person sees God and God in creation at least partially.

What we know and experience of God in this awakening is beyond words. It is the communication of God's excellence to a person's inner substance. This awesome revelation is one of terrible and solid array of divine power, but the lover who seeks God is made gentle and charming with all the gentleness and charm of creatures. Alone, one does not have the capacity and strength to deal with such an experience, for here the person faces God filled with the graces of all creatures, awesome in power, glory, and excellence. However, there is no longer fear, for God acts in a friendly way towards him or her. God reveals divine power with love and goodness. God communicates strength and love, admirable virtues, charity, knowledge of higher and lower substances, and transforms a person with the attributes of God.

Here God dwells within a spiritual seeker with an embrace that is close, intimate, interior, and pure. The person experiences this intimate embrace sometimes in enjoying God in quiet passivity, sometimes in an awakening when God communicates knowledge and love. Such a person should withdraw from all business matters and live in immense tranquility, so that nothing may disturb the union with the Beloved. However, in the act of striving to be perfect all is perfect, and the awakening and in-breathing of the Holy Spirit is strangely delightful. God breathes the Holy Spirit into the person and produces an awakening of divine knowledge, thus absorbing the individual in God and rousing love. This breathing of the Holy Spirit fills the person with good and glory and enkindles him or her in love of God, to whom be honor and glory forever and ever. Amen.

Reflections on stanza four

This final stanza of the *Living Flame of Love* describes how one gains an understanding of the whole cosmos in union with the love of the Word. The Lord of the world united to the entire cosmos graces us with love.

> How gently and lovingly
> you wake in my heart,
> where in secret you dwell alone;
> and in your sweet breathing,
> filled with good and glory,
> how tenderly you swell my heart with love.

The entire poem celebrates the divine gifts communicated in spiritual marriage. In this fourth stanza *the person is overwhelmed with deep love and thanks God for two gifts* in particular that manifest the indwelling of God. The first is an awakening of God in us that leads to a totally new vision of reality, and the second is an overflowing of God's love that makes it seem as if God is now breathing in us. This is a stanza of peace and gratitude. Instead of bursting forth in song, as in the previous verses, here one quietly celebrates the fullness of life experienced in this transformation.

In this stanza *the awakening refers to a newly gained awareness that love is the central value of life.* Generally people become captivated by the new awareness and live differently after the awakening. John tells us that this awakening is felt in our very substance, giving awareness of all the grace-filled wonders of the world and of every creature in perfect harmony. All the creatures of the world "disclose the beauties of their being, power, loveliness, and graces, . . . For the soul is conscious of how all creatures, earthly and heavenly, have their life, duration, and strength in Him" (F. 4.5). We see clearly how all creatures are distinct from God, but how they all can be understood better when viewed as part of God's being than in themselves. "And here lies the remarkable delight of this awakening: the soul knows creatures through God and not God through creatures" (F. 4.5).

This is God's gift, *a totally new vision of reality*; the revelation of the newness and harmony of the world in God. In this gift, the lover is awakened from a natural vision to a supernatural vision (F. 4.6). He or she, free from the veils that covered true sight, now sees both God and God-in-creatures in one moment's vision. It is like an awakening from sleep, achieved by the power of God's love within us. It is an awakening of God's excellence and power in one's inner substance; an awakening so overwhelming that one could not endure it had he or she not already gone through purification and had not God communicated this vision with friendliness, gentleness, and love. "Thus the soul experiences in Him as much gentleness and love as it does power and dominion and grandeur" (F. 4.12).

This communication of a vision of the cosmos in God is given in the depths of one's spirit, where God dwells in secret. The more a person has been purified the more God dwells within, feeling at home there, and the more the person longs to be alone with God, away from all other interests. In this awakening the lover's delight in experiencing God is so present it seems God is breathing within it. "And in that awakening, which is as though one were to awaken and breathe, the soul feels a strange delight in the breathing of the Holy Spirit in God" (F. 4.16). In this awakening of knowledge of God and the cosmos, we find that it is now the Holy Spirit who breathes new life within us, filling us with good and glory and enkindling within a profound love for God, "indescribably and incomprehensibly" (F. 4.17). Breath is life and without it we die. Sometimes a person who seems to be dying can receive artificial respiration and gain life again because someone breathes air into them. Sometimes people who have lost the ability to breathe on their own need to use a respirator. In this case God breathes new life into us and gives us chance to live in a new way we never expected.

John teaches us that love is the very reason why we were created (C. 29.3), the ultimate reason for everything in life (C. 38.5), and that at the end of life we will be judged on love (S. 60). The *Living Flame* teaches us about the priority of love in every aspect of life. The lover who has been searching for God thus sees that "love is proper to eternal life." However, it is also a very clear project of action for Christians in their lives and ministries throughout the world. So, God's love becomes a lamp illuminating all apostolic action and at the same time casts a protective shadow over love that assures its authenticity. We can describe the spiritual journey in several ways, but included among them is the understanding that our journey to God is the gradual acquisition and understanding of the nature of love. As we journey to God we perceive that love is the essential component of life. It is who God is, it is our own goal in life, and it is who we are meant to be.

Chapter 7
Feeling Oneself Lost in love
Reflections on a selection of John's poetry and prose

Five popular poems/gloss

Two special poems

Sayings of Light and Love

A ladder of love

John writes poetry spontaneously as a means of expressing, prolonging, and sharing his extraordinary experiences of loving union with God. He writes his commentaries at the request of his followers to explain and enlarge upon the concepts and teachings of the poems. When we read John's poems we can feel the depth of his feelings and experiences. When he describes God's love in salvation history but ends each enthusiastic proclamation with "although it is night," we can sense with him a little of his darkness and pain in the Toledan prison. When John was swept off his feet in Beas as he thought of God's beauty and then felt the need to add five stanzas to the *Spiritual Canticle* to express his mystical obsession with the beauty and love of God, we cannot but be swept into these feelings with him. John was often overwhelmed by his experiences of God's love, "fired with love's urgent longings." He tells God, "you have wounded me," "stolen my heart." He shares his unforgettable experiences with us all, inspiring us to pursue the love that was integral to every aspect of his life.

> C 27. There he gave me his breast;
> there he taught me a sweet and living knowledge;
> and I gave myself to him,
> keeping nothing back;
> there I promised to be his bride.
>
> 28. Now I occupy my soul
> and all my energy in his service;
> I no longer tend the herd,
> nor have I any other work
> now that my every act is love.

In many of his poems he seems lost in his love;

> 28. you will say I am lost;
> that stricken by love
> I lost myself, and was found.

Introduction

Language is so important to us for communication, development of relationships, and our own growth as human beings. It is particularly important in matters of religion where we transmit vital experiences through the language of faith. Sometimes expressions of faith end up as mere words, and we then lose the reality behind the words. So, when we seek to express spiritual realities we often use concepts from the Bible, church doctrine, speculative theology, even ideas from nature or other religions. For the mystic, all these are inadequate, for one cannot fully explain what one has experienced in God's loving gifts.

Conceptual and speculative language may help us to clarify and articulate our faith, but its vital core—our loving relationship with God—is more truly shared "in mystical theology which is known through love and by which these truths are not only known but at the same time enjoyed" (C. Prologue.3). People who have had a profound spiritual experience generally find it difficult to explain it to others in precise language. Often this is because they do not fully understand it themselves, or their explanation always seems to fall far short of the experience. John himself pointed this out, "everything I say is as far from reality as is a painting from the living object represented" (F. Prologue.1). But he also suggests, "For mystical wisdom, which comes through love. . . need not be understood distinctly in order to cause love and affection in the soul, for it is given according to the mode of faith through which we love God without understanding him" (C. Prologue.2). Because of this difficulty, mystics often use figurative expressions rather than rational explanations. Here we look at some of John's extraordinary writings—poetry and prose—that explore the depth of his love and experience of God and that challenge us to open ourselves to the call of love. Perhaps we too, like John, can feel overwhelmed in God's love and feel lost in this vision of love.

Five popular poems/gloss

John wrote five popular poems. "I entered into unknowing" is a poem of eight stanzas that describes an ecstasy experience in contemplation. This journey of unknowing transcends all knowledge. It is a further poetical description of the purification referred to in the *Ascent* (Bk II) and the culminating revelation of intimate knowledge that God reveals to those who love and strive for union.

Verse 3 catches both the longing and the overwhelming excitement of this journey to God.

3. I was so 'whelmed,
so absorbed and withdrawn, that my senses were left
deprived of all their sensing,
and my spirit was given
an understanding while not understanding,
transcending all knowledge.

"I live, but not in myself" describes how the soul suffers with longing to see God. It sounds like typical love songs of the day in which one longs to be with one's lover, transposed in this case to a soul's longing to be with God: "I cannot live without God." This present life is an imprisonment, "no life at all," in fact, "I pity myself, for I go on and on living"; "I am dying because I do not die." Partial experiences of God's presence, as in the Eucharist, help, but also remind one of the pain of absence "since I do not see you as I desire." The poem contains similar expressions of painful longing as we see in the *Spiritual Canticle* (stanzas 6-12), where John cries out: "Do not send me any more messengers." Even the little I see revealed leaves me dying "of, ah, I-do-not-know-what behind their stammerings." The bride describes the pain of "not living where you live." She feels wounded, her heart stolen, and left abandoned. As in the present poem, the bride in the *Spiritual Canticle* cries "reveal your presence" for "the sickness of love is not cured except by your very presence and image." But this comes only in eternity, when the soul can say "now I live because I do not die."

3. When I am away from you
what life can I have
except to endure
the bitterest death known?
I pity myself,
for I go on and on living,
dying because I do not die.

5. When I try to find relief
seeing you in the Sacrament,
I find this greatest sorrow:
I cannot enjoy you wholly.

all things are affliction
since I do not see you as I desire,
and I die because I do not die.

"I went out seeking love" substitutes the image of hunting for prey instead of longing for love. It is a secular poem to which John gives a religious interpretation (a lo divino). It describes the pursuit of love, "this adventuring in God." The motivation for this journey, this hunt, is love alone. However, John knows pains and darkness are part of this journey, "since I was seeking love the leap I made was blind and dark." John next refers to the method of the pursuit, "the higher I ascended . . . the lower and more subdued and abased I became." However, one must seek love "with unfaltering hope," "this seeking is my only hope." In a hunt, one pursues a future catch of prey, and in the spiritual hunt one refocuses life to purify hope. Seeking temporal love never satisfies but leads to frustration. But "the hope of heaven attains as much as it hopes for."

I went out seeking love, and with unfaltering hope
I flew so high, so high,
That I overtook the prey.

4. In a wonderful way
my one flight surpassed a thousand,
for the hope of heaven
attains as much as it hopes for;
this seeking is my only hope,
and in hoping, I made no mistake,
because I flew so high, so high
that I took the prey.

"Without support yet with support" describes one's attitudes and commitment in the spiritual journey. When one journeys "without support" of any created things one will then discover that he or she is "with support" of God. This is the journey of strong love, for it implies "living without light, in darkness." This short poem, to which John gives a religious interpretation (a lo divino), describes the disciple's longing for the love of God. The three stanzas successively focus on faith, hope, and charity. One's faith leads a person to abandon everything except the pursuit of God. One's hope for heaven gives meaning to this life. One's love turns everything to goodness, a delightful flame that transforms the whole of life.

> Without support yet with support,
> Living without light, in darkness,
> I am wholly being consumed.

> 3. After I have known it
> love works so in me
> that whether things go well or badly
> love turns them to one sweetness
> transforming the soul in itself.
> And so in its delighting flame
> Which I am feeling within me,
> swiftly, with nothing spared,
> I am wholly being consumed.

"Not for all beauty" is a secular poem that takes on extraordinary meaning for John who identifies beauty as the essence of God. Once a disciple has experienced the beauty of God nothing else will ever bring satisfaction. The main metaphor of the poem is food and eating and John compares all the delights of this world to those of "I-don't-know-what" of the next life. The former bring no satisfaction, "they tire the appetite and spoil the palate." This is because "He who is sick with love. . . finds his tastes so changed." He becomes sick of all creatures and cannot find contentment except in the Divinity. The poem describes "a person so in love, who takes no delight in all creation," but longs and hopes for a loving union beyond this world's limitations, "for I-don't-know-what which is so gladly found."

> 5. For when once the will
> is touched by God himself,

it cannot find contentment
except in the Divinity;
but since his Beauty is open
to faith alone, the will
tastes him in I-don't-know-what
Which is so gladly found.

6. Tell me, then, would you pity
a person so in love,
who takes no delight
in all creation;
alone, mind empty of form and figure,
finding no support or foothold,
he tastes there I-don't-know-what
which is so gladly found.

Two special poems

"A lone young shepherd" is a beautiful secular love poem that John transposes to a religious level (a lo divino). The shepherd is Christ and the shepherd-girl is humanity. Thus, the poem is an expression of the foundational story of Christianity: the good shepherd who gives his life for those he loves. His love is so strong he willingly lives in pain, "his heart an open wound with love." What brings pain to the shepherd is that in spite of his love for humanity, men and women frequently forget him, they ignore or draw away from his love, and they do not seek the joy of his presence. Nevertheless, his love continues, "he bows to brutal handling in a foreign land," and even goes to death on the cross to show his love. The poem describes the selfless love of the shepherd and gives no sign of the shepherd-girl's love. It is a reminder of how the shepherd-girl is redeemed from a loveless life by the redemptive love of the good shepherd.

1. A lone young shepherd lived in pain
withdrawn from pleasure and contentment,
his thoughts fixed on a shepherd-girl
his heart an open wound of love.

2. He weeps, but not from the wound of love,
there is no pain in such affliction,
even though the heart is pierced;
he weeps in knowing he's been forgotten.

5. After a long time he climbed a tree,
and spread his shining arms.
and hung by them and died,
His heart an open wound of love.

"For I know well the spring that flows and runs" is a particularly beautiful poem that describes the soul who rejoices in knowing God through faith. John wrote this poem while in prison in Toledo, probably around the octave of the feast of Corpus Christi. He had been deprived of the Eucharist for six months, living in his dark cell, with little light and overwhelmed by darkness. He can hear the rhythmic flowing of the river Tagus outside his cell. In this poem he professes his experience of God through faith in the Trinity; the Father—the eternal spring, without origin, whose bottomless love nurtures the world; the Son, "the stream that flows from this spring" and the Holy Spirit, "the stream proceeding from these two." Then John affirms that his entire faith in God is now expressed in the Eucharist, "this living bread for our life's sake," that satisfies us totally. He concludes "This living spring that I long for, I see in this bread of life." This is an expression of John's faith totally permeated by love. He weaves biblical themes of living water and bread of life throughout this beautiful doctrinal presentation. He ends each stanza with the insistent refrain "although it is night." He can satisfy his thirst for God "although living in darkness, because it is night." Night for John is guiding, transforming, tranquil, and leads to the union of the dawn.

10. It is here calling out to creatures
And they satisfy their thirst,
Although in darkness,
Because it is night.

11. This living spring that I long for
I see in this bread of life,
Although it is night.

Sayings of Light and Love

Among John's shorter prose compositions we find the *Sayings of Light and Love*, a collection of spiritual maxims that John used to give to his directees who then often copied them and passed them on to others. While written in prose there is a lyrical beauty about many of them. The structure of the sayings is very simple but not monotonous, and many are extraordinary in successfully condensing John's spiritual vision in a single statement. Some are quite poetical (number 16), some are maxims for life (60), advice in confronting dangers (66), or prayer (50). The major themes of the sayings are the necessity of spiritual direction, denial of one's appetites, the importance of being guided by reason rather than by feeling or taste, the nature of authentic love, and intimacy with God. One saying that is sometimes included with the others but not always is the "Prayer of a soul taken with love." This saying, which some writers consider autobiographical, develops in a continuing crescendo from the misery of sin, to humble abandonment, to confidence in Jesus, and finally to the enthusiastic possession of everything in the Lord.

John wrote these sayings on light and love because he felt motivated by love to do so, and he wrote them to speak to others' hearts and to stir them to greater love and service (*Sayings of Light and Love*, Prologue). John urges us to seek God with simple and pure love (2), in purity and single-mindedness (12), submissiveness (13), secrecy (20), urgency (32), and a complete focus on God's will (73) and Christ's cross (102). In order to journey in love, John says we need to be aware of our burdens and weaknesses (4), seek guidance for the journey (5), accept dryness and suffering (14), and move ahead with growing detachment (15, 43). We will need to focus every effort on God alone and take care of even small failures

(23), maintain our rootedness in God (39), keep distance from this world's business (58) and other people's affairs (61), and always leave aside what is not conducive to life with God (79).

Our journey to deeper love needs to be at God's pace without us becoming attached to our own goals or ways (40-41); we will need patience and a robust spirit (42), fortitude (95), attentiveness (44), constant purification (49), self-denial (51), a re-education of the faculties (55), and awareness of the next life (83) and final judgment (77). This great journey of life is an undertaking we pursue with patience (120), a contemplative spirit (121), and constant purification of imperfections (122). As we journey we must live in the presence of God (124, 142), with genuine self-surrender (128), always walking in solitude (136), with an unselfish heart (137). Thus we will be mindful of others and never speak badly of them (148), rather, speaking of them with kindness (151), and appreciating their gifts (47).

Since God loves us so much we must be forgiving of others (47), as we make our journey in God's company (53), giving priority to the love of God above all else (54). Daily we reflect on God's love and care (86), maintain confidence (89), and live in the presence of God (90). It is important that we practice frequent self-examination (105), accept whatever trials come our way (94), concentrating always on God's love (93). With enthusiasm for God (16) we must journey peacefully in tranquility (28), gentleness and patient humility (29), centering our lives on the Word of the Son (100) and imitation of him (157), realizing all we have has come from a loving God (108).

One of the especially beautiful and love-filled sayings is the "Prayer of a soul taken with love" in which the soul prays for God's help in the pursuit of love, knowing God will always be with the person who seeks love. The soul urges readers to start immediately in the pursuit of deeper love, to do everything for God's love, and to be singularly committed to discover the God of love.

The following are a few of the *Sayings* that focus particularly on love.

16. "O sweetest love of God, so little known, whoever has found this rich mine is at rest."

60. "When evening comes, you will be examined on love. Learn to love as God desires to be loved and abandon your own ways of acting."

68. "Take God for your bridegroom and friend and walk with him continually; and you will not sin and learn to love, and the things you must do will work out prosperously for you."

78. "If you desire that devotion be born in your spirit and that the love of God and the desire for divine things increase, cleanse your soul of every desire, attachment, and ambition in such a way that you have no concern about anything."

88. "Preserve a loving attentiveness to God with no desire to feel or understand any particular thing concerning him."

97. "The soul that walks in love neither tires others nor grows tired."

115. "Love consists not in feeling great things but in having great detachment and in suffering for the Beloved."

129. "The soul that has reached the union of love does not even experience the first motions of sin."

A ladder of love

Another way in which John synthesizes his system is his description of a life of love that develops in ten steps on a ladder of love. The steps on a ladder go up and also go down; we can ascend and descend with the same steps, gaining or losing height. As one ascends, one learns how to ascend more. As one descends and loses ground, one can descend even more. There are ten steps on this ladder of love. John calls knowledge of these steps "a science of love." This ladder of love presents the steps to follow to rise to God in love and union. You cannot remain stationary on this ladder; you either go up or you go down. This ladder describes the science of love. Climbing is always a challenge—you need preparation, courage, endurance, and perseverance.

This love of the ten steps transforms a person and fills him or her with love of neighbor too. John had an important guiding principle for all we do; "Where there is no love, put love, and you will draw out love" (L. 26). This ladder of love as a way to our destination is a wonderful opportunity to reaffirm our conviction that love is the gift, the motivation, the goal, and the reward of this journey. The pursuit of love leads to pain as we see more and more how much God deserves and how little we give.

John proposed ten steps in the "science of love," which he saw as a wonderful short way of reaching our destination. The first step on the ladder of love is when God gifts a person with the sense of dissatisfaction and sickness with the way things are going in life. The second step develops from the first and consists in a person's relentless pursuit of God, seeking only God in every aspect of life. The third step is when he or she performs good works as part of his or her total self-gift to God. The fourth step is an important development of love, for one now pursues God without fail, in spite of any sufferings that may come in the way. Step five on the ladder of love is when a person receives from God an impatient desire and an ardent longing for God.

The fifth step on the ladder of love leads into the sixth when the person's hope invigorates him or her to further purification and love in the pursuit of God. The seventh step is an ardent boldness when one is no longer satisfied with a moderate response to God and does not want to hold back development in any way, but receives courage to respond with boldness. The eighth step happens when a person is united to God in love even though not continually. In this intermittent, actual union, such a one now senses that he or she can reach out for God or be drawn to God by the infusion of love. The ninth step is when the Holy Spirit causes one to sense the presence of God's love in his or her life. It is a time of satisfaction in the blessings of God, and a person feels this is what he or she has been longing for—habitual union. The final step is one's union with God in afterlife, as he or she is totally purified and transformed by God's love. In a world that lacks love the pursuit of love requires courage. One does not climb this ladder with determination and effort. One must be receptive as one is drawn upwards by God's love. It is interesting that when mystics and spiritual writers of every generation are asked for the central value in the development of spiritual life, they emphasize love. These ten steps are our program of action in our journey through life.

John always seems to be on fire with his topic of God's love for us and our role and responsibility in this wonderful vision of love. The brilliance of John's poetry continues in the beautiful lyrical features of his commentaries, and both become sources of inspiration for readers. It is not an exaggeration to say that he conveys a sense of wonder and awe in the presentation of his works even before we consider the content. However, John does not just write such beautiful poetry because he is skillful and artistic. The beauty does not come from poetical insight but from mystical experience. He is writing about the most wonderful and beautiful experience of his life. John writes beautifully, not because he is a great poet but because he is sharing with us a wonderful mystical experience of God's love for the world and for each of us. It is interesting how one who has suffered so much is known for such beauty in his poetry and prose. John of the Cross is well known for the rigors of the spiritual journey and for the demands he makes on himself and on others in the pursuit of life with God. It is interesting that one who is so demanding also writes with such beauty and passion.

Chapter 8
Responding in love

In this final chapter I want to share a series practices that can help each of us build up a system of response in love. These are decisions that we consistently make to assure a life of love. We must avoid a merely believed-in love that is so common in contemporary spirituality. These are positive, active decisions that we make with God's help. We must have the courage to make these important decisions and persevere in the hope of love in spite of a world of hate.

1. Desire what God wants of us.

Our responding in love must begin by always desiring what God wants of us. We all know lots of people who want to dedicate themselves to God but they never get beyond their initial commitment. If we want to succeed then we must be always open to growth and be willing to take the whole costly journey to God. We must set ourselves a clear direction to follow and challenge ourselves to do what needs to be done to get there. We often say we want to pursue a deeper spiritual life and seek union with God, but we do not back up those desires with the necessary attitudes. We must match our longing with readiness to be drawn by God and must above all desire that God be everything for us. This will require of each of us education and sensitivity born of deep recollection, nurtured in silence; what John calls a "deep and delicate listening" (F. 3.34). This is a time when we who wish to pursue God give ourselves totally with fidelity and stability, wanting nothing except what God wants of us and doing nothing except what God wants from us. Only a total immersion in the desire for the will of God and longing for God's love will enable us to make this journey to spiritual life and enrichment. God must be everything to the person who seeks love and union. It is a fundamental attitude of directing the whole of life to God and centering all one does on God alone.

"What does it profit you to give God one thing if He asks of you another? Consider what God wants, and then do it" (S. 95).

2. Acknowledge there are fundamental disorders in our lives.

This is also a response of love. Our point of departure for the spiritual journey is awareness that we are born into a situation of disorder; our entire lives ought to be subordinated to the Spirit, but instead they go the other way, to sense. So, our response in love must include awareness of disorders in our lives and a willingness to change. More men and women are guided by sense than by spirit. The result of this natural decline is that we often hide our own true image, dignity, and finality, tend to continually regress instead of making progress, and even block divine interventions in our lives. We are surrounded by disorders; but, let us be clear, we cause these disorders because we are disordered people—we lack order or direction in our spiritual lives. We want to progress but at times we are unable to do so, in fact we even seem to be paralyzed. So, if we wish to make the journey to the love of God where alone we will find our authentic selves, then we must be willing to undertake the rigors of this journey. An essential aspect of our spiritual journey is the commitment to change and to transform ourselves with God's help into who we are capable of being. This process begins by removing disorders. Good intentions are not enough, and we can only get out of our disorders through complete purification. It is more difficult to discover disorders when they are the normal order of the day and everyone is involved in them. If we wish to respond in love we must face up to the disorders in our lives.

"The disordered soul possesses in its natural being the perfection that God bestowed when creating it" (A.1. 9.3).

3. Courageously choose a spirituality that will lead to the goals we seek.

We respond in love be dedicating ourselves to a spirituality that can attain the goals we seek. Often our spirituality provides a framework for our religious hopes, but does no more than indicate just how much further we need to journey. We live within a spiritual framework for years and even become shackled to it, but often we never see the goals we thought were ahead. For the most part in our spiritual lives we wander around, disoriented, until we conclude that the spiritual lives we live are inadequate, even artificial and will never help us attain the goals for which we long. There is nothing wrong with them—they are just not a recipe for success! John of the Cross presents us with an entire redoing of the spiritual system. He is not interested in any upgrades or additional improvements to what we have. For him, all outer changes are very secondary and are at the most aids in the inner transformation he wants for us. Nothing from the outside works; we must listen to what is within. Most people, even spiritually dedicated, dabble in spirituality. John wants us to give a clear focus to our spiritual lives and then pursue that vision and goal relentlessly. Spirituality can never be just a segment of our lives; it is a way of living our entire personal and community reality. Our response in love must be serious.

"Some people—and it is sad to see them—work and tire themselves greatly, and yet go backward; they look for progress in what brings no progress but instead hinders them. Others in peace and tranquility, continue to advance well" (A. Prologue 7).

4. Focus on spiritual life especially as a journey of love.

Clearly our journey to God is based on faith, but faith alone is not enough for spiritual development must include an emphasis on responses of love. The journey of love includes an anxious search for the love of God with all the painful longings that are part of this journey, followed by the joy of encounter with its accompanying preoccupation at the possibility of future loss. The journey then moves on to total union with the joy and benefits of this love, and finally further intense desire for union in glory. If the journey of faith is the purification of our knowledge of God and of our ways of knowing God, then the journey of love is the purification of our love of God and of our ways of loving God. During this journey of love we will have three different experiences, all contributions to our ways of loving God. First, there is the love of absence: when God seems absent from us, we can experience God's transcendence. Second, there is the love of union: in union we will feel God present in everything and find that true love is participation. This is a time to experience God's love and goodness. Third, there is the experience of absence even when we are in union. In loving union we realize our own insufficiencies and unworthiness, anxiety rises, and we feel absence at a deeper level even though we are in union, for the union is not permanent. We cannot control the stages but we definitely want to make our spiritual journey a journey of love.

"[L]ove alone, which at this period burns by soliciting the heart for the Beloved, is what guides and moves it and makes it soar to God in an unknown way along the road of solitude" (N.2. 25.4).

5. Stress the importance of contemplation in our journey to God.

The key step on our journey to God is the transition from activity when we think we are achieving everything to the passivity of contemplative prayer when we allow God to work freely within us. Our responses in love are God's work within us. If we wish to be prayerful people who can live with purpose in our pursuit of love then we need to be people of deep reflection, and we call such people contemplatives. We contribute our efforts, but if there is any success it is because God is drawing us. Let us remind ourselves what it means to be contemplative. Contemplatives are persons who are comfortable with themselves, at ease with their own strengths and weaknesses, and yearn to identify who they are capable of being. Contemplatives are not afraid to be alone, isolated from others for a while in silence, emptiness, and stillness. Contemplatives are people with a sense of purpose, free from distracting and disintegrating secondary values. Their lives are unified in one great commitment to the vision they pursue. Contemplatives appreciate anything that is beautiful: people, senses, music, art, literature, or drama. Contemplatives are skillful in finding opportunities to reflect, either spontaneously while out in the country or in parks, or by deliberately preparing a part of their home to be conducive to a reflective experience. Contemplatives know the importance of the body for quality reflection and prayer. They take diet and exercise seriously and appreciate that the Christian tradition of fasting can have a healthy impact on a life that is reflective. Contemplation needs nourishing with ongoing education in values, complemented with good literature of all kinds and an awareness of contemporary world events. Growth is a gift, and we do no more than prepare ourselves to receive the gift. Authenticity is found in the center of ourselves; not by having more or doing more but by being more. Contemplation is God's transforming work within us and will influence our lives on many levels. These responses of love are God's gifts within us.

"Through this contemplation, God teaches the soul secretly and instructs it in the perfection of love without its doing anything or understanding how this happens" (N.2. 5. 1).

6. Strive to be everyday mystics.

As Christians who are ready for the future centered on love we must be mystics—people who have a genuine experience of God. If we are people of interiority and faith, our Christian spiritual experience will flow from personal experiences of God's mercy, forgiveness, compassion, and love. This is the only way to access love. This experience of faith leads us to live with a sense of wonder, appreciating that the whole of life is aflame with the presence of God. However, life in the Spirit is nurtured in solitude, where we reaffirm faith and re-experience what we believe in. As believers, our experience of God produces the life of faith and hope that results from and causes love. After all, mysticism means not knowing, but experiencing that God is love. It gives rise to a passionate love for life, beauty, and wisdom, a thirsting for life itself—a power that drives us to union. Thus, spirituality, the mystical experience of the living God, is the level of our faith, hope, and love that as Christians we live and foster in others. The call to become a mystic, an ordinary, everyday mystic, is the most important challenge of our lives. Having experienced God's love, we then find that this love demands action on behalf of others everywhere. So, our efforts to be everyday mystics is a daily pilgrimage of response in love that also requires us to show courage and determination in extending love to others.

"Take God for your . . . friend, and walk with him continually; and you will not sin and will learn to love, and the things you must do will work out prosperously for you" (S. 68).

7. Live in the darkness where we will find light.

As we move ahead to immerse ourselves in the life of love to which God calls us, we will find that we must not be afraid of emptiness and darkness, for life is better in darkness when we can appreciate our own emptiness. What we should be concerned about is the fullness and illumination we think we already have, for they do not lead us to God. We look but do not see. Sometimes it seems we will never get out of the darkness—as John said, we move from darkness to darkness guided by darkness. Everything changes when we encounter God in darkness. Alone we are helpless, but with God as our light we can move through darkness. When we enter darkness in pursuit of God, life becomes better. We can look back and see that living in dark times was a wonderful experience, for the night can be dark, but it can also be guiding, more lovely than the dawn, a time to encounter one's lover. It is darkness that brings illumination; that thick darkness where God dwells (Exodus 20:21). The thought of living, learning, and growing in darkness seems so strange to us. But, John of the Cross disrupts our way of thinking, valuing, viewing religion, and understanding our own destiny. To be in darkness does not mean that you cannot see or that you have no vision. It is a call to see in a new way and to look at things in a new way. In darkness God can break through our selfish defenses and bring us genuine illumination. Darkness fosters the absolute conviction of divine transcendence. Our spiritual lives can always be enriched by the dawn that follows the dark night of contemplation.

John encourages us when we walk in "these darknesses and voids of spiritual poverty," but he tells us "nothing is failing you." "Do not worry, but be glad." "You were never better off than now," "God does one a great favor when he darkens the faculties and impoverishes the soul." "God is leading you by a road most suitable for you." "Desire no other path than this" (Ls. 11 and 19).

8. Make sure that love motivate us in everything we do.

We pray for God's help in the pursuit of love, knowing God will always be with us when we seek deeper love and long to respond in love. We can try to do everything for the love of God, and dedicate ourselves totally to the discovery of the God of love. Sometimes we think our sins hold us back, or that God is reluctant to grant us this gift of love. We might even think God is waiting for our good works or that God desires to see greater commitment on our part to the acceptance of the sufferings that lead to love. Then again we remember that there is no reason for God to wait, we are not earning anything, everything is gift anyway. We cannot free ourselves from lowly ways of loving unless God achieves this for us. In this great gift of love God gives us everything else. If we become hardhearted because of self-love we start a process of self-degradation and become ever more coldhearted and cannot get out of it without God's help. If we are aflame with love we become soft and gentle, meek, humble, and patient. In the evening of life we will be judged on our love, and so we should learn to love as God desires, for one who loves never grows tired in his or her dedication. "The love of God in the pure and simple soul is almost continually in act" (S. 54). Love will be the motivation for all further stages in this exciting journey. We all want to journey in life "along the spiritual road that leads to the perfect union with God through love" (N. Title). Of course, one only undertakes this journey when one is "fired with love's urgent longings," and one travels "with no other light or guide than the one that burned in my heart." At the end of the journey, it is "love alone," that makes one soar to God (N.2. 25.4). Perhaps we could describe the spiritual life as the journey of strong love (N.2. 11.3; see C. 31.4). From start to end John's approach is to affirm "nor have I any other work now that my every act is love" (C. v. 28), and overriding every other conviction is "When evening comes you will be examined in love" (S. 60). Let us make sure that love motivates us in everything we do.

"*O great God of love, and Lord! How many riches do you place in the soul that neither loves nor is satisfied except in you alone, for you give yourself to it and become one with it through love*" (L. 11).

9. Learn how to listen.

As we focus our attention on God we must choose what to listen to, so that we are not distracted by our cluttered world. We need a mature focus on what priorities we choose to pursue. This means deliberately choosing what we will set our hearts on, what we will tolerate, what we will heed. Clearly in all of this, we must listen to our hearts, for God speaks to our hearts. This includes living detached from all that is not God. We also listen to God's messengers in our inner spirit, to those who share our values, to creation that reveals traces of God's presence, to others who teach a thousand graceful things of God. When we listen carefully, all tell us something about God, the divine presence in our world, and the unceasing divine love that calls, heals, challenges, and fulfills. "God teaches the soul very quietly and secretly" (C. 39.12). In fact, God communicates in silence. Often, humanity cannot or will not listen, but God's communication is everywhere. As an English hymn reminds us, "The whole world is aflame with God but only they who see take off their shoes." We must foster a sense of solitude, and in that solitude hunger for true silence. We must leave aside everything from the outside and only listen to what is within. In silent attentiveness and inner recollection, we open our hearts to the transforming presence of God. When we open our hearts and listen we find God in the world, in others, in divine wisdom and designs. We discover God's love for us and we become thrilled to find God teaches us how to love, and we enjoy a silent resting in the Spirit. In silent resting we can prepare our hearts to discover both God and the love we long for. Transformation comes in silence. In fruitful emptiness God guides our spiritual activity. If we wish to respond in love we must learn how to listen.

"God speaks to the heart in this solitude . . . in supreme peace and tranquility, while the soul listens" (F. 3.34). "He whom my soul loves is within me" (C. 1.9)

10. Value solitude and silence.

The pursuit of transformation and union with God implies seeking life beyond this one that gives meaning to our existence. Hence, we should have solitude in our lives aware that this world and its values are passing away. Thus, we pay no heed to this world unless it prepares us for the next. Moreover, there are advantages to be gained from withdrawal from idle gossip, useless encounters, unnecessary business interactions, frivolous entertainment, and so on. We must create space in which prayer and union with God take precedence. We must also allow ourselves to be drawn to God in solitude on a daily basis. Solitude does not mean we are unfaithful to the duties of daily life. Rather, we must fulfill them responsibly. In all our daily activities we should maintain recollection, be focused, and do all in the presence of God. Our lives and culture are filled with noise and distractions of all kinds. It seems no one values silence. Yet all spiritual traditions speak of the importance of silence and of the temptations to be found in incessant noise and distractions. We learn nothing from constant noise, but silence presents us with opportunities for reflection, self-discovery, and openness to the call of God. Silence is one of those basic qualities that nurture other important aspects of our lives. Without silence we can neither foster contemplation nor a reflective approach to activity. Those who love silence respond with gentleness. We must treasure silence, find a quiet place both materially and in our own hearts. We need quiet time and a special place to listen to the whispers of the Holy Spirit. Valuing solitude and silence is a response in love.

"A person accomplishes a lot by learning to do nothing" (F. 3. 47).

11. Seek God with determination and perseverance.

At times God seems hidden, but we must go in search of God knowing God is always in search of us. "The good contemplative must seek him with love" (C. 1.6). Certainly, we find God in the revelation of the Son. "The Son is the only delight of the Father, who rests nowhere else nor is present in any other than in his beloved Son" (C. 1.5). In addition to the Son's revelations, the primary experience in which the Trinity is discoverable is in the depths of our own hearts. "It should be known that the Word, the Son of God, together with the Father and the Holy Spirit, is hidden by his essence and his presence in the innermost being of the soul" (C. 1.6). God is within everyone by divine essence. God is never absent from us, for in each of us there is a center which is naturally divine. Also, God is even hidden in the divine gifts of presence, whether by essence, grace, or spiritual affection. Even these are hidden, for "God does not reveal himself as he is, since the conditions of this life will not allow such a manifestation" (C. 11.3). God's hiding place is within us not outside us; "you yourself are his dwelling and his secret inner room and hiding place" (C. 1.7). So, we should not go searching for God elsewhere, outside of ourselves, but find God within. Nearness to God inflames greater love, reveals the divine life, but reminds one God is more hidden than revealed (see C. 13.1). No matter our own efforts, God remains hidden, and we need to appreciate the need for purification, emptiness, and receptivity. We find God still hidden in faith, and we continue to seek God in faith, love, and unknowing, leaving aside all former knowledge, understanding, activities of faculties, and satisfactions. We must always seek God with determination and perseverance.

"Only by means of faith, in divine light exceeding all understanding, does God manifest Himself to the soul" (A.2. 9.1).

12. Find identity beyond suffering.

John saw his sufferings in prison in Toledo as darkness before the dawn, a glad night that led to transformation in love. As he welcomed his transformative sufferings, John became a different person because of suffering. Christians have always believed in the redemptive value of suffering when linked to love, and Christians of every age give a special authority to suffering for love. It is a beautiful response in love. John had no interest in suffering for its own sake. On the contrary, contemporaries affirm that he had a very pleasant personality, enjoyed life and people, loved the outdoors, and delighted in friendships. John also practiced discretion in austerities and criticized those who "burden themselves with extraordinary penances" (A.1. 8.4). However, he pursued love and was willing to do whatever was necessary to achieve his goal; this is a fundamental pillar of John's vision of life. Again, suffering is for love, and when motivated by love "you will not notice whether you suffer or not" (L. 17). So, a person finds his or her own identity beyond suffering and only because of suffering. One's authentic calling can be appreciated only in suffering which becomes the beginning of a newness of life. When suffering is the result not of love but of hatred, then each one must confront it, remove it, never forget it, and respond to it in love and service. John gives the impression that if a person is not pursuing love in facing life's sufferings then he or she is involved in something that is part of the failures and unfaithfulness of this world. Acceptance of suffering is integral to our response in love.

"What profit is there in anything that is not the love of God?" (A.3. 30.5).

13. Long for the healing presence of God.

We all experience pain in our spiritual journey from feeling that our efforts are getting us nowhere and from our inability to sort things out. We run here and there seeking solutions, and we discover that God alone can heal and guide us. However, God attracts us and then leaves us incomplete and painfully dissatisfied. We find life needs total love, and we long to give God our complete love. This means constantly longing for God and never being satisfied in anything other than God. We will always be restless until we rest peacefully in God's love of us and our love of God. Only a life directed to God can bring us fulfillment in life, and our daily strivings for union are our way of asking God to show us divine love. St. Augustine wrote that our hearts are always restless until they rest in God. Sure enough in our spiritual journey we frequently experience a love-sickness that results from having tasted the goodness of God and finding that our longings remain unfulfilled and our love incomplete. It seems God steals our hearts and leaves us helpless and without the loving response we expected. We find nothing else satisfies us, and we lose taste for anything else. We leave aside all self-interest and seek deeper union in any way we can. But only God's healing presence and transforming love can satisfy us. We long for the wholeness that only a life of dedication to God can bring. Without this it seems we are living in darkness. It is always helpful to identify our own longings for fulfillment and discover they are met in God alone. Life can be full of wearying and annoying distractions that can only be overcome with the refreshing presence of God in our hearts. Love happens within us when we focus ourselves entirely on God's healing love.

"The sickness of love is not cured except by your very presence and image, [O Lord]" (C. 11. 12).

14. Refocus knowledge, memories, and desires on faith, hope, and charity.

One of the most important responses of love is centered on the theological virtues of faith, hope, and charity. The spiritual journey to God is sometimes described as a journey of faith, or a journey of love, or the seeking of God through the nights to union. It is also possible to see the whole spiritual journey as the purification, redirection, and transformation of the spiritual faculties of intellect, memory, and will. People who dedicate themselves to God generally think they know God, possess God, and love God, but this knowledge, possession, and love is so far from authentic that it is damaging to one's pursuit of God. The intellect can accumulate knowledge, the memory can gather all its wonderful images, and the will can focus on its many loves, but together these do not correspond to God. The work of purifying these faculties begins in the active night of sense. The three spiritual faculties suffer when they are empty, but they must be emptied of false values in order to be filled with new ways of knowing, possessing, and loving God. When they are empty and purified they feel intense pain at their own emptiness and yearn for what they lack, namely God. The intellect thirsts for divine wisdom. The will hungers for the perfection of love. The memory seeks the possession of God in hope. The intellect, memory, and will must turn away from their normal objects of knowledge, possessions, and loves to focus instead on faith, hope, and love. We know more about God in faith than in the accumulation of knowledge. We possess God more in hope than we do in memories. We love God more in charity than we do in accumulated desires and small loves.

The spiritual journey implies emptying ourselves of all that is not God, so we can attain what is truly of God.

> *"[T]he soul is not united with God in this life through understanding, or through enjoyment, or through imagination, or through any other sense; but only faith, hope and charity (according to the intellect, memory, and will) can unite the soul with God in this life" (A.2. 6.1).*

15. Never give in to a reduced ideal of our calling.

"Those who truly love God must strive not to fail in this love" (C. 13.12). We often live an illusion that the life we are living is all there is. However, we must get ready for a call we never thought we would receive. We will always be restless until we rest in the love of God. John gives us hope in his call to transformation. He tells us what can happen to humanity under the transforming power of God's love. We all struggle with our personal pain and longing to be who we are called to be—to be our best selves. The fathers of the Church defined a human being as "capax dei," capable of God. We are all called to search for union with God. In doing so we will discover God and we will also discover ourselves. This journey will always imply collapsing habits from the past, living in faith, abandoning what we previously thought worked and now know does not, and journeying to the unknown.

We can make this journey with confidence for it is not our arduous undertaking, scrambling to take a few steps forward. Rather, we are being drawn by the love of God who is always the "primary Lover." This transformation is God's work, and we surrender to the divine action within us. We cannot achieve it, but we can prevent it from happening. When God wishes to send us "truth and love," all we can do is say "My heart is ready, O God, my heart is ready" (Ps. 56). We must match God's gift of selfless love with our own choice to focus exclusively on a life of love. This will be a painful journey for God does not love like we do, and our journey is learning how to love as God wills. There is only one major commitment that a human being can make, to pursue a life of love with the knowledge that nothing else matters. This is the one great loving response we must make.

"You can truthfully call God Beloved when you are wholly with him, do not allow your heart attachment to anything outside of him, and thereby ordinarily center your mind on him" (C. 1.13).

16. Appreciate God's steadfast love for each of us.

Our world does not seem to have much interest in God and certainly does not think God has much interest in us. Many seek God, but the wrong god—distant, angry, and violent. The fundamental conviction of Christianity is that God is close to us and loves us in such a way that God takes a risk with us. When God sees the world drifting away from divine union in love, God acts unceasingly to bring us back and hold us close in love. A hymn describes this response, "O Love that will not let me go." However, we evidence a lot of conscious and unconscious resistance to God's love and illumination, and we need purification of our actual, habitual, and social sins before we can appreciate that God is love and calls us to a life of union in love. Every day, each one of us can proclaim, "I will sing of thy steadfast love, O Lord, for ever" (Psalm 89: 1). "A soul enkindled with love is a gentle, meek, humble, and patient soul" (S. 29). We must tell ourselves that the human heart that seeks meaning and fulfillment can only find them in love.

"Nothing is obtained from God except by love" (C. 1 13).

17. Practice both patience and urgency.

We will need patience on our spiritual journey, lots of it! because slow maturing is an essential aspect of human growth. We will need to be patient in continuing to make daily efforts with equal enthusiasm even when we never seem to be getting anywhere. On the other hand, patience is not enough; time will not have a magical effect in spiritual growth. We must make constant effort; effort with a sense of urgency and fidelity will be a daily need. John pointed out that those who lack patience "grow angry with themselves in an unhumble impatience. So impatient are they about these imperfections that they want to become saints in a day" (N.1. 5.3). On the other hand many people have too much patience when dealing with the spiritual life and spend years without making any significant progress. So, while these two qualities at first seem opposed, they are not. Both are indispensable, and can mutually correct each other and maintain our commitment in balance. We must be patient to be where God wants us to be, and always filled with a sense of urgency to move towards deeper union in love.

"[Many beginners] do not have the patience to wait until God gives them what they need when he so desires" (N.1. 5.3). Others "are so patient about their desire for advancement that God would prefer to see them a little less so" (N.1. 5.3).

18. Let love alone condition everything we do.

John teaches us that love is the very reason why we were created (C. 29.3), the ultimate reason for everything in life (C. 38.5), and that at the end of life we will be judged on love (S. 60). We must maintain the priority of love in every aspect of life throughout our spiritual journey. Whenever we think about the qualities of God we find that God reveals divine love in the communication of every divine characteristic. God loves with the full force of each of the divine attributes and with all of them influencing each other. Thus, God loves each of us with justice, goodness, mercy, and so on. When we seek to know and experience God, we discover that God's personal love for us is imbued with every one of the divine attributes. The person thus sees that "love is proper to eternal life." We can describe the spiritual journey in several ways, but included among them is the understanding that our journey to God is the gradual acquisition and understanding of the nature of love. As we journey to God we perceive that love is the essential component of life. We remind ourselves that we are created in the image and likeness of God who is love.

The major transformation of love in contemplation empowers a person to see the whole world through the lens of love. In our contemporary world where a continued lack of love threatens to burst frozen hearts, John's vision of a world dedicated to love is revolutionary. John has a guiding principle for all we do; "Where there is no love, put love, and you will draw out love" (L. 26). "The ultimate reason for everything is love" (C. 38.5).

"Stricken by love . . . I lost myself and was found" (C. v. 29).

19. Be enthusiastic about life with God.

Let us respond in love with enthusiasm. We are people transformed by faith, and the most immediate consequence of faith is our conviction that there is more in life than meets the eye; there is a world that is not immediately apparent. Our experience of faith teaches us that there are two horizons to life and they are intimately linked. We discover in ourselves a zone that naturally yearns for transcendent reality, and we live at this level of mystery, where we are enthralled by enduring truths. Everything we think and do is transformed by this awareness of a relationship between our everyday life and a realm of life that gives meaning to this one. Again, here, life is judged and given a new meaning by a transcendent horizon of life. We need to pay attention to the connections between our own yearnings for fulfillment and the call of another realm of life. As we journey through life we catch a glimpse of a horizon of life beyond this one. This is one of the foundational experiences of our spirituality. The world in which we live only has meaning because of a realm of life of which we catch sight from time to time. We are not journeying in the unknown, even when we journey through the dark nights, for we can still feel a certain companionship of our God who draws us to divine life (N.2. 11.7).

"I no longer live within myself and I cannot live without God,
for having neither him nor myself what will life be? It will be a
thousand deaths, longing for my true life and dying because I do not
die" (Stanzas of the soul that suffers with longing to see God, v. 1).

20. Our mission in life is to respond in love

John's life reveals the same commitment to love as do his
writings. Let us imitate him. (Chapter 1) God's self-revelation
teaches us that the essence of life is a union of love, and so we
model our lives and world on God's love. (Chapter 2) Our
preparations for authentic fulfillment in life center on freeing
ourselves from false loves and learning new way of loving based on
God's example. This is our major responsibility in life. (Chapter 3)
Our journey in life in the companionship of God follows the steps
in the ever deeper union of two lovers—a journey that fills us with
thrill and excitement. Love must motivate us in everything we do.
(Chapter 4) This love must be strong to accept any pain that will
lead to the transformation we seek. (Chapter 5) We pursue a life
which consists in our immersion in love, an awakening to a new
way of living when God lives and breathes in us and in all we do.
This is our new vision of life. (Chapter 6) We find our true selves
when we become lost in love for we were created for love. (Chapter
7) Our mission now is to respond in love.

Notes

1. Arthur Symons, "The Poetry of Santa Teresa and San Juan de la Cruz," *The Contemporary Review*, 75 (1899); 546.

2. Xavier Pikaza, "Amore de Dios y contemplación Cristiana: Introdución a San Juan de la Cruz," *Actes III*, p. 53.

3. Colin Thompson, *St. John of the Cross: Songs in the Night* (Washington, DC: Catholic University Press of America, 2003), p. 55.

4. See Thompson, p.277.

Other Books By Leonard Doohan

STUDIES OF THE MAJOR WORKS OF JOHN OF THE CROSS

This series presents introductions to each of the great works of John of the Cross. Each volume is a study guide to one of John's major works and gives all the necessary background for anyone who wishes to approach this great spiritual writer with appropriate preparation in order to reap the benefits of one of the most challenging figures in the history of spirituality. Each book is a complete introduction offering background, history, knowledge, insight, and theological and spiritual analysis for anyone who wishes to immerse himself or herself into the spiritual vision of John of the Cross.

While targeted to the general reader these volumes would be helpful to anyone who is interested in the spiritual guidance of this saint. These books give insight into the critical components of spiritual life and can be helpful for anyone interested in his or her own spiritual journey. They could be helpful for the many people involved in the spiritual guidance of others, whether in spiritual direction, retreat work, chaplaincy, and other such ministries. Throughout these books the reader is encouraged to develop the necessary attitudes, enthusiasm, spiritual sensitivity, and contemplative spirit needed to benefit from these spiritual masterpieces of John of the Cross. Attentive reflection on these studies will encourage readers to have a genuine love for John of the Cross and his approach to the spiritual journey.

These books give historical, regional, and religious background rarely found in other introductory books on John of the Cross. They each present an abbreviated and accessible form of John's great works. Later chapters in each book give John's theological and spiritual insights that could be used for personal reflection and group discussion. Sections abound in quotes and references from John's books and each sub-section can be used as the basis for daily meditation. The volumes complement each other, and together give the reader excellent foundation for reading the works of this great spiritual leader and saint.

Volume 1. John of the Cross: Your Spiritual Guide

This unique book is written as if John of the Cross is speaking directly to the reader. It is a presentation by John of the Cross of seven sessions to a reader who has expressed interest in John's life and teachings. This book introduces the great mystic and his teachings to his reader and to all individuals who yearn for a deeper commitment in their spiritual lives and consider that John could be the person who can guide them.

Table of contents

1. John's life as a contemporary life
2. John as a spiritual guide
3. John's vision of the spiritual life
4. Preparations for the spiritual journey
5. Major moments and decisions in the spiritual life
6. Necessary attitudes during the spiritual journey
7. Celebrating the goal of the spiritual journey

Volume 2. The Dark Night is Our Only Light: A Study of the Book of the Dark Night by John of the Cross

This introduction to the Dark Night of the Soul by John of the Cross gives all the necessary background for anyone who wishes to approach this great spiritual work with appropriate preparation in order to reap the benefits of one of the most challenging works in the history of spirituality. The book starts with the life of John of the Cross, identifying the dark nights of his own life. It provides the needed historical, religious, and personal background to appreciate and locate its content. It then presents readers with aids they can use to understand the work. With these preparations in mind the book moves on to present the stages of the spiritual life and the importance of the nights. A summary of John's own work brings readers in direct contact with the challenges of the message and its application today. The book ends with 20 key questions that often arise when someone reads this book.

Table of contents

Volume 3. The Spiritual Canticle: The Encounter of Two Lovers. An Introduction to the Book of the Spiritual Canticle by John of the Cross

The book starts with the life of John of the Cross, showing how he was always a model of love in his own life, and how, guided by his own experience he became a teacher and later a poet of human and divine love. The book provides the needed historical, religious, and personal background to appreciate and locate its content. The book then presents the links between John's Spiritual Canticle and Scripture's love poem, the Song of Songs. A summary of John's own work brings readers in direct contact with the challenges of the message and its application today. With these preparations in mind the book moves on to present the stages of the spiritual life and the importance of the journey of love. The book then focuses on key concepts in the Spiritual Canticle, applying each of them to contemporary situations. Finally it considers the images of God presented in the book and how they relate to the spiritual journey.

Table of contents

Volume 4. John of the Cross: The Living Flame of Love

The Living Flame of Love is the final chapter in John's vision of love. It describes the end of a journey that began in longings of love that became an experience of purification for the person seeking union. The Living Flame of Love picks up from the final stage of union in the love of spiritual marriage and describes, in great beauty, several aspects of this final stage in the union of love. All these ideas are part of John's wonderful vision of love. Many writers have emphasized the spiritual value of a life of love, but John's vision is more expansive and integrated than approaches presented by anyone else.

Table of contents

A Year with St. John of the Cross: 365 Daily Readings and Reflections

This book, A Year with St. John of the Cross, offers 365 daily readings and reflections. In this year with St. John of the Cross we will read and reflect on his life, ministry, spiritual direction, spirituality, as well as selections from all his works, short and long. The readings and reflections in this book will introduce readers to all these, as well as comments from many leading writers and commentators on John. This year will be an opportunity for readers to immerse themselves in the spirituality of John of the Cross. Each day offers a focused reading, four key reflections, and three specific challenges for the day.

For those who are enthusiastic supporters of St. John of the Cross, and for others who wish to discover new and substantial paths in their spiritual journey, this book is a one-of-a-kind opportunity to encounter John and his challenges like never before. Let your reading of this new book be your personal journey with John of the Cross, to a deeper union with God. One of the main uses of the book is to help readers who do not have ready access to a spiritual director. Maybe these readings and reflections will help. I hope you will find this special book helpful in your spiritual journey.

BOOKS ON SPIRITUAL LEADERSHIP

How to Become a Great Spiritual Leader: Ten Steps and a Hundred Suggestions

This is a book for daily meditation. It has a single focus—how to become a great spiritual leader. It is a book on the spirituality of a leader's personal life. It presumes that leadership is a vocation, and that it results from an inner transformation. The book proposes ten steps that individuals can take to enable this process of transformation, and a hundred suggestions to make this transformation real and lasting. It is a unique book in the literature on leadership.

This book is the third in a series on leadership. The first, Spiritual Leadership: The Quest for Integrity gave the foundations of leadership today. The second, Courageous Hope: The Call of Leadership, gave the contemporary characteristics and qualities of leadership. This third book focuses on the spirituality of the leader.

Courageous Hope: The Call of Leadership

This book's focus on leadership and hope is very appropriate given today's climate of distrust that many find results in a sense of hopelessness in their current leaders. Individuals and organizations are desperate for leaders of hope. Many books on leadership point to the need for inner motivation, but that inner motivation must be hope in new possibilities for a changed future. It is hope that gives a meaningful expression to leadership and enables the leader to be creative in dealing with the present. More than anything else it is a vision of hope that can excite and empower leaders to inspire others to strive for a common vision.

"Doohan strengthens our resolve. He restores our hope. And in an echo of Robert Frost, he is not only a teacher, but an awakener. May this book find you in a place where your will to grow is matched by an inner radiance to serve and help heal those around you... the reading will meet you there and the end result will be a gift to the world." Shann Ray Ferch, PhD., MFA Professor and Chair, Doctoral Program in Leadership Studies, Gonzaga University. Editor, International Journal of Servant Leadership.

"Read every word of this book. Leaders stuck in the past, afraid to face the future, afraid to take a risk because they might be wrong need an infusion of Courageous Hope. People are not looking for a simple, blind-faith hope. They are looking for leaders with a deeper understanding of hope as described in this book." Mary McFarland, PhD., Professor, and Former Dean of undergraduate through doctoral programs in Leadership. International consultant in leadership and education.

"Ask people who were alive during the Great Depression what a huge difference Franklin Roosevelt made in their lives by giving them reasons to be hopeful. Ask people who were alive during the papacy of John XXIII what they loved most about him, and chances are they'll say that "good Pope John" gave them hope for the future. Read Courageous Hope and learn how to be that kind of leader yourself." Mitch Finley, Author of over 30 award winning books.

⍰

Spiritual Leadership: The Quest for Integrity

In eight clear and challenging chapters, the reader is invited to partake of a rich menu of reflections on the meaning of spiritual leadership and how it can transform one's role in the workplace, ensuring a collaborative environment of trust and confidence that energizes not only the culture of an organization, but also the effective accomplishment of its mission.

Leonard Doohan's highly readable book presents leadership as a call motivated by faith and love that results in a change of life, a conversion, and a breakthrough to a new vision of one's role in the world.

"Leonard Doohan's Spiritual Leadership is a profound and caring work . . . I highly recommend it to anyone interested in the spiritual meaning of servant leadership." Larry C. Spears.

"'The leader within,' . . . is well served by Leonard Doohan's book, Spiritual Leadership. It is a profound guidebook for leaders of the future, who live their values, who keep the faith." Frances Hesselbein. Chairman, Leader to Leader Institute

"Dr. Leonard Doohan's new volume on Spiritual Leadership reaches beyond, or perhaps better, beneath the many current volumes on leadership which emphasize skill sets, techniques, and learned habits." Robert J. Spitzer, SJ, PhD. President and CEO, Magis Institute

BOOKS ON CONTEMPORARY SPIRITUALITY FOR CHRISTIAN ADULTS

Embrace the new enthusiasm in the Church and nurture your Christian commitment with weekly reflection.

A new spirit is stirring in the Church. We must overcome the failures of the past and prepare ourselves for a future of growth and responsibility. Let us rekindle spiritual insight, accept our spiritual destiny, and refocus on the essential teaching of salvation. While many have left the institutional churches, and sadly may never return, perhaps the challenge to renewal of Pope Francis may re-attract them to the essentials of Christian commitment. The Church will grow and benefit from an informed laity who deepens knowledge of the essential teachings of faith. I created a book with short sections, targeting areas of personal reflection valuable for individuals and discussion groups for this purpose. Read a section each week and gain a new strategy for nurturing your spiritual life.

⍰

Rediscovering Jesus' Priorities

This book urges readers to look again at Jesus' teachings and identify the major priorities. It is a call to rethink the essential components of a living and vital Christianity and a challenge to rediscover the basic values Jesus proclaimed. Use the book for a short meditation and personal examination, as a self-guided retreat to call yourself to renewed dedication to Jesus' call, or for group discussion and renewed application of Jesus' teachings.

Ten Strategies to Nurture Our Spiritual Lives: Don't Stand Still—Nurture the Life Within You

This book presents ten key steps or strategies to support and express the faith of those individuals who seek to deepen their spirituality through personal commitment and group growth. These ten key components of spirituality enable dedicated adults to bring out the meaning of their faith and to facilitate their spiritual growth. It offers a program of reflection, discussion, planning, journaling, strategizing, and sharing.

The One Thing Necessary: The Transforming Power of Christian Love.

This radical new interpretation of love as the touchstone of the Christian message, explores the human longing for meaning; the Scriptures; the relational model of the Trinity: the ideas of human vocation, destiny and community; the mystical spiritual traditions; and his own experiences to explain what love is, how we find it, and how it can change the world. Each of the seven chapters contains several quotes and focus points at the beginning and provocative questions at the end for reflection or discussion by adult religious education and bible study groups.

"This book is all about love—and love as the one thing necessary. It is most certainly not about easy love or cheap grace. It is about the transforming power of Christian love. It is not only challenging but disturbing, a book written with conviction and passion."

Fr. Wilfrid Harrington, OP., Biblical scholar.

"[Doohan's] artful gathering and arranging of ideas reminds one of the impact of a gigantic bouquet of mixed flowers chosen individually and with great care." Carol Blank, Top 1000 reviewers, USA.

"Would that we heard more about this in our churches and religious discussions because, "this transforming power of Christian love will save the world" (p. 93). Mary S. Sheridan, "Spirit and Life."

ANNOUNCING A NEW BOOK

Growth In Christian Faith: Struggles, Glimpses Of Grace, Life And Fulfillment

This short book deals with some of the many concerns that people have today regarding their life of faith. There are three parts to the book. First, the book considers some of the many struggles that people must overcome in order to continue as people of faith. Nowadays, it is hard to believe and certainly difficult to distinguish between authentic faith and the clutter of secondary beliefs that confuse and misdirect people's dedication and enthusiasm. So many believers put their energy into issues that were not primary concerns for Jesus. It is no use denying the problems we face in our society and churches. Rather, we must struggle to grow in faith in spite of the difficulties all around us—whether the growing irrelevance of religion, the worrying trends of social movements that simply use religious language for their political and social goals, or the politicizing of religion. We will have to purify these developments if faith is to survive. Second, if faith is to grow we will need to search for reasons to believe, consciously identifying those experiences that we see as glimpses of grace that strengthen faith. We often find that life is full of small things that we are convinced matter intensely, and passionately, and convincingly. These experiences give us hope and when shared in community strengthen our dedication, illumine our faith, and deepen our love in God's self-communication. Third, in re-committing ourselves to the life that results from faith we nurture that life and discover that God in whom we believe draws us to a greater share in divine life through spiritual growth, deeper prayer, participation in the life of the Church, enriching energies of the soul, and deeper union with the Son, our Lord Jesus Christ.

So, part I faces the struggles that challenge our faith, part II encourages us to keep focused on convincing reasons for faith, and part III insists we can find life and fulfillment in our dedication to God. I hope readers will find this book helpful in their own journeys to deeper faith.

All books are available from amazon.com

Comment on the author's blog at
johnofthecrosstoday.wordpress.com

Visit the author's website at leonarddoohan.com

www.ingramcontent.com/pod-product-compliance
Lightning Source LLC
LaVergne TN
LVHW011230080426
835509LV00005B/426